LIORA BELS

THE MIX

A LOVING BLEND OF PLANT-BASED RECIPES

Photographs by Mirjam Knickriem

teNeues

"I'VE LEARNED THAT

PEOPLE WILL FORGET WHAT YOU SAID,

PEOPLE WILL FORGET WHAT YOU DID,

BUT PEOPLE WILL NEVER FORGET HOW

YOU MADE THEM FEEL."

MAYA ANGELOU

(1 9 2 8 - 2 0 1 4)

DEDICATION

I dedicate this book to my roots: my dearly beloved parents, who filled my life with unconditional warmth and love, who taught me about values, and who made my journey possible. I am blessed, as I am a child of love. My gratitude is endless.

My dad always said to me, "Knowledge is wealth." It's being able to learn, to travel and see the world, to collect visual and emotional memories, and above all to feel and experience life with all your senses. This wealth is something you can't lose, no one can take it away from you, and it has no price. It's within you and becomes part of everything you are. So my parents always encouraged me to see the world, to live and love, to feel and to breathe everything in deeply. With gratitude.

From the depth of my heart I thank my parents for all those possibilities—to grow, to learn, to be courageous and yet mindful.

Looking at my roots I see my crown—my children. The now, the future. They teach and remind me to see the world through a child's eyes, to slow down once in a while, and to experience everything around me with mindfulness and enjoy it with fascination.

This is to life.

TABLE OF CONTENTS

I LOVE THE
EMOTIONAL ASPECT
OF FOOD. IT NOT
ONLY NURTURES
YOU BUT ALSO
BRINGS PEOPLE
TOGETHER, IT
MAKES YOU FALL
IN LOVE AND THE
TASTE AND SCENT
OF IT CREATES
MEMORIES. FOOD
MAKES YOU FEEL.

INTRODUCTION

This book is about pleasure, the joy of eating, and the culinary celebration of the wonderful produce nature has to offer. It focuses on aesthetically refined plant-based cuisine, using only fresh, flavorful, sensual, and nutrient-dense foods in their least processed state.

Natural food is a gift from the earth to us. I feel that we need to respect that gift, nurture it, and nurture ourselves with gratitude and love. And I'm convinced we will see and feel the difference.

It's a blessing to live in a world where whole, plant-based foods are not only abundant, but are also the most beneficial way to eat for our body and mind. Healthy choices can be incorporated into everybody's lifestyle no matter what dietary preferences they may have.

In conversations about food or eating a more healthy plant-based diet, I am often confronted with the words "no time," "no ideas," "no talent," "don't know how to cook," "lack of inspiration." As a working mom, I understand the challenges of finding the time to cook an abundant, healthy meal or to make real changes in your cooking, yet we all appreciate the importance of providing our families and ourselves with thoughtfully prepared, tasty, and nourishing food.

I truly believe that you don't have to be a chef to cook a delicious, wholesome meal made with high-quality organic products. This is why I created recipes that are easy and quick to make—without having to sacrifice nutrients, taste, and aesthetics.

I love food and want to create a scrumptious, beautiful, vibrant, and healthy cuisine—one that is fun, indulgent, and inspiring and that can create substantial changes in the way we feel and look. The recipes in this book are all mainly made in a high-speed blender, some use a food processor, and others are made by simply using your hands—quick and easy. Perfect for everyday life.

These recipes are inspired by my travels, by different cultures, nature, farmer's markets, my childhood, architecture and design, and all forms of creative expression. Colors, aromas, and tastes move me deeply and these passions are reflected in my culinary creations. Sometimes I will pick a classic recipe and transform it into a new one by using alternative natural and nutritious products; other times I will simply be inspired by nature's bounty to invent new blends and combinations. Developing and preparing recipes is a process I very much enjoy. From carefully choosing the right ingredients to combining the tastes, textures, and colors that best showcase the beauty and aesthetics of the food, it's always about the senses.

I have put all my passion into this book—I have built a deep love affair with natural food and my wish is that I inspire you to make the best possible food choices for you and your family every day. I hope that the combination of taste, aesthetics, and insight about the countless benefits that I share with you becomes the key to incorporating more natural foods into your daily nutrition. I hope you enjoy this food journey and find guidance, inspiration, and the love for a whole-food, plant-based cuisine.

This book is made for everyone!

MY FOOD PHILOSOPHY

I love natural food and I am deeply fascinated by the emotional aspect of eating a healthy cuisine. The beauty of nutrition, the aromas, natural colors, and how the aesthetic allure of refined cooking works to spark our emotions—all of this enchants me.

During my childhood, the kitchen was the place where it all happened. My beloved dad was a wonderful hobby chef, a virtuoso in the kitchen. He was all about taste, texture and freshness, and he was deeply passionate about experimenting with ingredients. He celebrated eating with joy and pleasure—and with his passion for making a mess in the kitchen! But what influenced me the most was his philosophy that food not only nurtures, but also brings people together, that it can make you fall in love and that the taste and scent of it create memories. It can bring us back to our childhood, remind us of special moments, make us dream. Spices may even inspire us to take trips to faraway places.

I believe that wholesome food has a tremendous impact on our bodies, minds, and on our lives in so many wonderful ways. It's very important to make time to listen to your body instead of just following trends that suggest that there is only one right way to eat or live. There is no specific eating plan that suits everyone the same way. It's not about labels or about counting calories, and it's certainly not about restriction or following a "diet" for a certain period of time.

My personal food philosophy has a beginning and no end. It's about abundance, pleasure, and the celebration of the wonderful produce nature has to offer: whole, organic, plant-based foods in their least processed state combined to create a healthy, vibrant, and delicious cuisine.

I believe in a holistic, balanced approach to life. By creating daily rituals of eating nourishing foods, adding more plants to your diet, sleeping well, incorporating stress management, and working out in the way that's right for you, you can create a sustainable positive effect on your life today and in the future. The benefits of a healthy routine are truly limitless.

Since the field of nutrition is always developing and changing, I am constantly trying to learn and grow with it, to widen my knowledge about healthful food, the art of eating well, and living a conscious life. My intention is to reflect and to incorporate this in my wholesome recipes and lifestyle. This is truly an exciting, interesting, and delicious journey that I am happy and grateful to share with you.

INSIDE MY KITCHEN

ABOUT THIS BOOK

This book serves as an inspiration for, and a guide to, preparing nutritious, fresh, and vibrant plant-based whole food that is delicious and makes you feel happy and good.

The recipes are easy to use, approachable, and adaptable to your lifestyle, needs, and taste preferences. So feel free to adjust ingredients to taste, experiment, and have fun in the kitchen. You can mix and match recipes, and exchange grains, legumes, nuts, and seeds if you desire to add more variety to your weekly nutrition.

Choose organic and fresh foods in their least processed state whenever possible. The source and production process of foods are important if you're looking for both health benefits and taste.

You might need to adjust ingredient amounts according to the high-speed blender you're using; since they come in different sizes, container shapes, and capacities, you might need to add more liquid or dry ingredients to achieve friction.

Usually these recipes can serve one to three, but of course that's entirely up to you and your appetite, and the purpose of the meal.

TECHNIQUES

On Blending

Blending your food has wonderful benefits: it is a good way to provide your body with the nutrients it needs in an easy, fast, and practical manner. You can add lots of leafy greens, vegetables, and a whole meal's worth of fruit and all the fiber stays in your blend. The blending process makes your food easy to digest, as chewing is no longer needed. Hence, smoothies or shakes, for example, are also great for your workout: your body does not have to expend as much energy for digestion after a strenuous workout, so it can concentrate more on recovery. The liquid texture also helps your body absorb nutrients better. I recommend using a high-speed blender like a Vitamix for the creamiest, smoothest results.

On Soaking

Soaking your grains, legumes, raw nuts, and raw seeds has great benefits: all of these foods contain naturally occurring substances like phytates and enzyme inhibitors that prevent them from sprouting and protect them against insects and other predators. They are not beneficial for us, though. Phytic acid, for example, can interfere with our absorption of minerals. By soaking grains, legumes, nuts, and seeds, we remove or neutralize these substances so our own enzymes can work properly and our bodies can better absorb all the wonderful nutrients. Further, soaking greatly aids digestion. I also find it enhances the natural flavor and reduces the cooking time of grains and legumes.

You can find instructions and the different soaking times for grains, legumes, nuts, and seeds on the following pages.

EQUIPMENT AND UTENSILS

Most of the recipes in this book require a high-speed blender to produce the creamiest and richest textures. You might be able to use a regular blender for some recipes but I highly recommend a blender with more power for the best results. I love my Vitamix and use it on a daily basis—it truly is a great investment. Other than that you can use a food processor for some recipes or even just your hands. A good knife can always be of great use as well. For making all the delicious plant milks in this book you will need a nut milk bag.

THE
BEAUTY
OF
FOOD

STOCKING THE PANTRY

NUTS AND SEEDS

I love to incorporate nuts and seeds into my recipes; they are so versatile, nourishing, and delicious. I mainly use them for nut milks—I make my own almond milk (page 44) almost daily—but I also use them for baked goods, dips, and dressings; for toppings on soups, salads, and stews; for homemade nut or seed butters (page 106), or simply as a snack. I find that cashews or macadamia nuts make an amazingly delicious dairy replacement. My favorite recipes using cashews are Cashew Yogurt Bowl (page 64) and Cashew Sour Cream (page 138). My favorite macadamia nut recipe is the divine Macadamia Vanilla Ricotta (page 100).

When buying nuts and seeds, always look for raw, unsalted, organic options. They have higher nutritional value and are free of potentially harmful chemicals. For freshness and a longer shelf life I suggest storing all nuts and seeds in airtight glass containers in the refrigerator.

I recommend soaking your nuts and seeds before using them. Simply cover them with warm water, add 1 teaspoon of sea salt and let soak. See the chart for soaking times. If you want to keep soaked nuts and seeds ready for use you will need to dry them after soaking using a dehydrator to return them to a crisp state. Store them in the refrigerator in airtight glass jars for when you need them.

SOAKING TIMES FOR RAW NUTS AND SEEDS

Almonds	8–12 hours, or overnight
Cashews	4–6 hours
Hazelnuts	6–8 hours
Macadamia Nuts	8–12 hours
Pecans	6–8 hours
Pistachios	8 hours
Walnuts	6–8 hours
Chia seeds	8–12 hours, or overnight
Flax seeds	8–12 hours, or overnight
Pumpkin seeds	6–8 hours
Sesame seeds	4–6 hours
Sunflower seeds	2–6 hours

NUT AND SEED BUTTERS

If you purchase nut or seed butter, make sure you buy organic, unsweetened, and unsalted products. If possible, look for raw spreads since their healthy fatty acids tend to change when being processed or heated up and they lose important nutrients during the process. I recommend making your own homemade nut and seed butters, which is simply amazing—it's so easy and quick and you know what's inside. Plus you can choose your own combinations and blends (see page 106). One of my favorite recipes is the indulgent Heavenly Chocolate Butter (page 104).

Note: Making your own nut or seed butter does not require soaking, but roasting. Roasting will not enhance the absorption of their nutrients, as soaking does, but it makes them easier to digest.

LEGUMES

Legumes are truly food for the soul. They are nourishing and warm the belly and the heart. In a plant-based diet, lentils, beans, and peas are the typical go-to foods when you're looking for a high protein intake. Not only do they provide your body with a wide range of beneficial minerals and proteins, but they are also high in satiating fiber, which is valuable for digestion and boosts energy levels.

I love to incorporate legumes into my meals and use them in soups and salads or to make deliciously creamy dips and hummus. As with grains and pseudo-grains, I recommend soaking legumes for great benefits, such as supporting digestion and improving nutrient absorption (see page 17). To soak legumes, rinse them well and then place them in a container, cover them with water, and add 1 tablespoon of lemon juice. Let soak for 8 to 12 hours, or overnight, then drain and rinse well before cooking. Store all sorts of legumes in airtight containers and place them in a cool place away from direct sunlight. Stay away from canned options always and opt for organic products.

Beans

Beans are packed with nourishing proteins that support bone and skin tissue, speed up your metabolism, and maintain muscle growth. They are also an excellent source of vitamin C, which helps strengthen our immune system. Due to their wonderful load of fiber, they can aid in regulating blood sugar levels.

You will find a wide range of beans available in the shops. Dark red kidney beans and black beans are among the most common, and both go well in salads or stews. Garbanzo beans (chickpeas) are popular in falafel, hummus, soups, and stews. Because of their buttery texture, lima beans or "butter beans" are one of my favorites to use for deliciously creamy side dishes. Another great, tasty option for salads, stews, and soups are easily digestible mung beans.

Beans, especially chickpeas, are a delicious addition to the Classic Tomato Soup (page 118)—filling and nourishing.

Lentils

When it comes to lentils, it is truly hard to get bored! Lentils are not only supertasty and great for your daily dose of protein, they also provide your body with many outstanding nutrients such as folate. Folate is said to support your nervous system and brain function, and is crucial during pregnancy to reduce the risk of certain birth defects.

There are various kinds of lentils on the market, each of them perfect for certain dishes. I love beluga or le Puy lentils as a delicious and healthy ingredient for salads, soups, and side dishes, as they tend to maintain their shape after cooking. If you cannot find these in your health food store, however, regular French green lentils make a great substitute. Yellow and red lentils are wonderful for any kind of soup, stew, or dal since they cook quickly and have a creamy texture and thus are easily pureed. Lentils are a fantastic addition to the Cashew Curry Cream (page 144)—one of my favorite dishes in this book.

Peas

I. Love. Peas. Their sweet taste, their starchy texture, and their fantastic color just make me happy! Peas contain lots of valuable vitamins and important minerals, such as iron, magnesium, potassium, and folate, all amazing for maintaining your immune system. Folate is especially crucial during pregnancy, as it supports healthy cell production in the fetus. Plus, the fiber in peas is good for digestion as well as controlling blood sugar and cholesterol levels. Besides containing a beneficial ratio of omega-3 and omega-6 fatty acids, peas also offer a lot of healthy protein; if you pair them with a whole grain like quinoa or millet you will easily obtain the full range of essential amino acids your body needs.

I use peas not only in salads, soups, and stews but also in dips. One of my favorite pea recipes is Pea Pistachio Party (page 126).

Note: If you buy fresh peas, look for firm pods and a strong green color. Frozen peas are just as good as fresh peas and you can use them in just the same way.

WHOLE GRAINS

I love to incorporate whole grains into my daily menu. The variety is so generous and the uses are so varied: from adding them to salads, soups, and stews to using them in baked goods or creating delicious breakfasts, it just never gets boring. Below is a list of my favorite grains. Should you have a gluten intolerance or suffer from celiac disease you will be happy to see a great variety of delicious gluten-free options.

Look for high-quality, organic products whenever possible for a nutrient-rich outcome. To prolong their shelf life, place whole grains in an airtight container and store in a cool, dry place.

I recommend soaking grains for great benefits (see page 17). To soak whole grains, rinse them well and then place them in a container, cover them with water, and add 1 tablespoon of lemon juice. Let soak for 8 to 12 hours, or overnight, then drain and rinse well before cooking.

GLUTEN-FREE

Amaranth

Amaranth contains more nutrients than you might think. During the times of the Incas and Aztecs, amaranth was worshipped as a nourishing powerhouse! And for a good reason: this tiny pseudo-grain is a great source of fiber, is easy to digest, and contains a good amount of lysine, an amino acid that is very important for building skin, muscle tissue, and bone. Lysine also supports absorption of calcium, magnesium and iron, all of which are found in amaranth and which provide your body with many health benefits.

With its nutty and earthy taste, amaranth is a great addition not only to sweet dishes like porridge and granola, but also to savory ones like stews and soups. It also works well in combination with other "grains" like quinoa. Give it a try!

Buckwheat

Despite its name, buckwheat is a so-called pseudo-grain and is closely related to the vegetable rhubarb. Pseudo-grains are not actual grains but are in fact seeds that can easily be used as an excellent, gluten-free alternative to your usual grains. Buckwheat is a good source of the flavonoid rutin, which has wonderful antioxidant properties and various anti-inflammatory effects. This "grain" is also high in enzymes, proteins, and minerals such as iron and magnesium that can help regulate your blood sugar and cholesterol level and support cardiovascular function. Its high amount of fiber may improve digestion.

Millet

Using millet as a base for your dishes can be a wonderful way of providing your body with important minerals, vitamins, antioxidants, and plant-based proteins. It is a good source of important nutrients, including copper and magnesium, B vitamins and fiber. Millet can also act as a valuable prebiotic inside your gut by feeding healthy microflora and supporting digestion. It is one of the few grains with alkalizing effects and is fantastic for your overall health. Although millet belongs to the pseudo-grain family and is technically a seed, you can use it in the same way as any other grain; for example in salads or, sweetened with honey and cinnamon, as a tasty alternative to your usual morning porridge.

Stores usually offer yellow millet; however, it naturally also occurs in red, white, and gray varieties.

Quinoa

As a highly nutritious pseudo-grain, quinoa does not belong to the whole grain family but is a type of seed. Called "Mother Grain" by the Incas, quinoa serves as a rich, complete protein source, meaning it contains all nine essential amino acids (amino acids that cannot be produced by your body and therefore have to be incorporated into your diet). It is especially high in the amino acid lysine, which is linked to muscle growth and is believed to speed up your metabolism. Quinoa also provides you with a good amount of fiber to support digestion and keep you full for a longer period of time. Minerals like manganese, magnesium, iron, and potassium help sustain energy levels and flavonoids (a group of plant metabolites acting as antioxidants) may boost your immune system. Since it ranks low on the glycemic index, quinoa is believed to promote healthy blood sugar levels. Quinoa is very versatile—it is great in savory dishes with veggies and a delicious Spicy Tahini Sauce (page 136), for example or sweetened as a warming, soft quinoa porridge. I simply love quinoa!

Rolled Oats

Being an amazing source of calcium, magnesium, potassium, and especially protein, oats are popular among athletes for good reason. Calcium supports bone density and strong teeth, magnesium and protein help grow and maintain muscle tissue and nerve function, and potassium is great for an overall healthy cardiovascular system.

Oats also contain a significant amount of vital antioxidants, which are beneficial for healthy cells. Plus, having oats in the morning is not only a delicious start into the day, but may increase mental concentration and leave you full for longer thanks to their high fiber content. I love to eat overnight oats in the morning—one of my favorite recipes is Tahini Overnight Oats (page 86). Rolled oats are actually whole grains, softened and pressed to flatten during their processing. They are also wonderful to use in cookies or any other baked goods.

Note: Oats are naturally gluten-free. During their processing, however, they are likely to become contaminated by gluten-containing grains handled in the same facility. To make sure your oats do not contain any gluten, look for those with a gluten-free label.

Whole-Grain Rice

Whole-grain rice is a fundamental part of many cuisines since it acts as a filling, nutrient-rich fuel for the body. It provides your body with a wide spectrum of complex carbohydrates that are great for lasting vitality throughout the day. But there's more to rice than just that: whole-grain rice contains significant amounts of healthy fiber, which supports digestion, and great amounts of protein that are vital for your bones and muscles and support regenerative processes in the body. On top of that, whole-grain rice is a fantastic source of magnesium and vitamin B, both essential for a strong immune system and healthy blood cell production.

I always go for whole-grain options, as all valuable, natural nutrients in rice are found in the bran. White rice has had its bran removed and therefore loses about half of its precious nutrients.

I love incorporating brown rice and other whole-grain rices (such as black rice and red rice) into my meals due to their nutty flavor, and whole-grain jasmine rice can be a great option for many delicious exotic dishes such as curries. In Southeast Asia, black rice pudding is popular for breakfast, as it is said to be packed with healthy antioxidants.

GLUTEN-CONTAINING

Barley

Another fantastic way to pump up your daily meals in a delicious and nourishing way is barley. Barley scores high as a valuable whole grain and has been consumed by people around the globe for thousands of years due to its amazing health benefits. This grain contains valuable vitamins and minerals that can greatly support your immune system and boost your overall well-being. By providing your body with astounding amounts of fiber, barley can also help smooth digestion and prevent your blood sugar from spiking to unhealthy levels after a meal.

You can find different types of barley: whole hulled barley, which is considered a whole grain and lightly pearled, or completely pearled barley, which means the outer bran has been removed and along with it its wonderful nutrients; pearled barley is technically a refined grain and not considered whole. As with rice, the less pearled the grain is, the more nutrients it contains. That's why I would advise buying the hulled option, if you have the choice. A good indicator for the nutrient richness of the grain is its color; the darker the grain, the more nourishing it is.

Barley can be a great addition to soups and stews, where it adds a creamy texture. Other great options include using it as a simple, earthy base in various salads or meals, or simply serving it as a side dish along with steamed or roasted vegetables.

Spelt

With its slightly sweet and nutty flavor, spelt makes a great alternative to wheat in many baked dishes such as breads, pies, and muffins. The grain beats wheat not only in its nutrient density but also in its heightened digestibility, as its fiber is highly water-soluble. Soluble fiber is believed to have various beneficial qualities such as regulating cholesterol and blood sugar levels, which makes spelt an excellent option for diabetics. Spelt is also a great source of vitamin B3 and important minerals such as zinc, iron, and magnesium.

You will be impressed by this grain's versatility: you can use it as a wonderful substitute for rice, for example in risotto, or make luscious desserts out of spelt semolina.

If you use spelt flour for baking, there's only one catch to remember: your baked treasures may dry out a bit quicker than those made with wheat flour.

FLOUR

Here's a variety of my favorite flours to use. All happen to be gluten-free. Some flours are great on their own; others, like coconut flour, should be used in combination with other flours for the best results.

Make sure you store flour in an airtight container away from sunlight. If you have enough space in the fridge, you may want to consider placing it there, as cooling will slow down the oxidation process and will protect it from going rancid too quickly. If you try the flour and find it to taste bitter, it has gone bad.

Almond Flour & Almond Meal

I love almonds in all forms. They are tasty, so full of goodness, and so versatile! Almonds are not only a great and superdelicious source of protein but are also high in health-promoting fats that help your cells receive all the essential nutrients they need. They are a rich source of the antioxidant vitamin E, which gives your immune system a little boost and may help protect your cells. On top of that, almonds have alkalizing effects, and due to their good amount of fiber they can even balance your digestion.

When it comes to baking, you want to be aware of the difference between almond flour and almond meal: almond flour is blanched, finely ground, and can easily be added to all kinds of baked goods like cakes, breads, or muffins. Almond meal, on the other hand, is prepared from almonds with skins and has a coarser grind; I sometimes like to add it to breads, for example. Just as with coconut flour, it is best to combine almond meal with other flours due to its texture.

Buckwheat Flour

Buckwheat flour is one of my favorite ingredients for baking. I just love its nutty, earthy, rich flavor. I truly believe it is one of the most beneficial options in a gluten-free diet because of its highly nourishing content of antioxidants, proteins, and minerals, and its versatility. As buckwheat is a valuable source of magnesium, iron, and the flavonoid rutin, using buckwheat flour in your recipes may also be an excellent way to boost your energy levels and support your immune system. Because of its high fiber content, buckwheat is easily digestible, and since it is said to help stabilize blood sugar levels instead of shooting them up, it can be seen as a really healthy and smart alternative to wheat-based products.

I like to use buckwheat flour for breads, pancakes, or Blinis (page 186), or my beloved Banana Bread (page 178). You have to try it—it's so good!

Coconut Flour

To me, anything made from coconut is a good choice. That's why I find coconut flour to be another fantastic option for people following a gluten- or grain-free diet. Since the flour is low in sugar and carbohydrates it scores pretty low on the glycemic index and won't spike your blood sugar levels.

Coconut flour is made from dried ground-up coconut flesh and can be found in most health food stores. Don't get distracted by its name; it is actually nut-free and therefore suitable for allergy sufferers. The best thing about coconut flour, though, is not only its mild yet superdelicious coconutty flavor, but that it is especially high in fiber and protein. Coconut flesh is a true nutritional powerhouse, containing a bunch of great vitamins, healthy fatty acids, and minerals. All of them are essential for good immunity, a healthy metabolism, and solid energy levels.

This rather exotic, fluffy flour option has a dry texture that lacks elasticity and generally won't work too well in most baked goods on its own. That's why I recommend using it in combination with other flours rather than on its own as a straight substitute.

Teff Flour

Teff is another great option if you are looking for an alternative to your usual gluten-containing grains. The tiny grains are the seeds of a type of grass native to Ethiopia and Eritrea. I discovered teff not too long ago and I've become a huge fan. I believe the name speaks for itself: the plant that yields teff seeds is called "lovegrass"—and a little more love (or teff) in our lives can't hurt!

Teff grains come in various colors, from a mild and chestnutty tasting white to a darker brown that tastes like yummy hazelnuts. Although they are really tiny, they contain a huge amount of fiber, which can help stabilize blood sugar levels and ease digestion. Teff is also rich in protein and lysine (an essential amino acid that our bodies need but can't produce, and that we therefore have to take in through our diet). It is said to support muscle tissue and mineral absorption. Besides lysine, teff provides you with wonderful amounts of calcium, phosphorus, copper, and vitamin B, which are said to be beneficial for brain health, the cardiovascular system, skin and muscle tissue, and good metabolism.

Teff flour is the pulverized form of teff and can be used in various ways. When you bake with it, keep in mind that teff flour won't rise as much as wheat flour, so your end result might lack its usual height (but will be full of healthy nutrients instead). Ethiopians use the flour to create a wonderful porridge, but you can also use it to make pancakes and wraps, thicken your soup, or simply add it to other tasty bowl dishes.

Teff flour can usually be bought in health food shops. As always, I advise you to buy an organic product to avoid potential chemicals in your food and to obtain the highest amounts of nutrients.

FATS

Fats are a very important ingredient in my diet and I use them generously. Although many people still believe that fats are bad for them, some fats actually have incredibly beneficial properties that are amazing for our health, metabolism, and overall well-being.

Of course it is important to use the right fats for the right purposes. Some oils are good for cooking, while others are much better for refining meals by drizzling on the dish. Oils that are in their raw form, meaning they are "virgin" and unrefined, have a low smoke point and should not be heated above that (particular) point, as they contain delicate nutrients that get destroyed when cooked and may form harmful free radicals. Fats with a higher smoke point can easily be heated without oxidizing quickly.

These are three of my favorite oils, the ones I use on a daily basis for cooking and refining dishes.

Coconut Oil

Coconut oil is truly dear to my heart. I indulge in its texture, its taste, and its scent. It is a versatile and genuine natural powerhouse, a superfood indeed—for inner nourishment and external beauty care.

Coconut oil has incredible health benefits. About half of the fatty acid content in coconut oil is lauric acid, a medium-chain triglyceride (MCT) which is also an important component in human breast milk. Your body converts lauric acid to monolaurin, which has strong antiviral, antifungal, and antimicrobial properties and is believed to support the immune system.

But there's more to be said about this wonderful remedy: the MCTs in coconut oil are rapidly transformed to energy by your liver, and thus give your metabolism a quick boost. On top of that, this exotic oil can also help lower cholesterol and support healthy blood sugar levels. Its nourishing qualities also serve your skin: applying coconut oil externally has hydrating, nourishing, and soothing benefits. And oil pulling (swishing 1 tablespoon of oil in your mouth for several minutes) with coconut oil is fantastic for improving oral health and dental hygiene, because of its antibacterial properties. I use it for everything from head to toe.

Good to know: There are many different methods of extracting coconut oil and thus different types, qualities, and aromas.

For most of my recipes that don't require high-heat cooking, I use exclusively organic virgin or extra-virgin coconut oil for the most nutritional benefits. I like to add this high-quality oil to raw foods, such as smoothies, and to warm dishes as a garnish. When purchasing raw coconut oil always check the label of the bottle and look for "virgin" or "extra-virgin." For cooking, roasting, and baking at high temperatures I use organic expeller-pressed non-hydrogenated coconut oil, which is extracted at low temperatures without chemicals. This oil has a higher smoke point and is thus far less likely to cause free radical formation inside your system when heated. Even though this type of coconut oil is not in its raw form, it is still considered a healthy oil and a better alternative to other refined oils.

By the way, if you live in a country where it's not always warm, the oil will get solid. You might have to heat it up in a warm water bath before use.

Hemp Oil

Packed with essential omega-6 and omega-3 fatty acids in a beneficial 3:1 ratio, hemp oil is one of your best oil options for a healthy and balanced diet. Its polyunsaturated fats are believed to help regulate cholesterol, blood sugar, and hormone levels; boost your immune system; and kick-start your metabolism for more energy throughout the day. Plus, the oil's inherent antioxidants—vitamin E and beta-carotene—are thought to be beneficial for your nervous system.

Good-quality hemp oil should be dark in color, cold-pressed and unrefined with a fresh, nutty aroma; I recommend purchasing only an all-organic product in a dark glass bottle. Hemp oil is very sensitive to heat and light so store it inside your refrigerator. It is not recommended to use hemp oil for cooking; using it raw preserves all its valuable nutrients.

Good to know: If you combine hemp oil with coconut oil, it will help your body absorb its rich content of omega-3.

Olive Oil

Due to its manifold health benefits, its wonderful flavor, and its origin, olive oil is one of the key ingredients in Mediterranean cuisine. Its healthy, monounsaturated fats support your cardiovascular system, help regulate cholesterol levels, and provide your body with wonderful nutrients like vitamin E, vitamin K, and omega-9 fatty acids.

Olive oil also contains natural preservatives and antioxidants that are simply great for your cells and overall well-being. Maybe the buoyant spirit of the Mediterranean cultures is rooted in their dear olive oil—it is said to have mood-lifting qualities!

I recommend buying only organic unrefined cold-pressed extra-virgin olive oil that comes in a dark glass container. It should have a strong aroma similar to freshly picked olives and herbs. Like hemp oil, extra-virgin olive oil should be used in its raw form to preserve all its valuable nutrients. It is not recommended for cooking, as it has a low smoke point and is very sensitive to heat. Hence, you should store extra-virgin olive oil in your refrigerator and use it up within two months.

SWEETENERS

You can add a bit of sweetness to your meals without having to use refined sugars and artificial sweeteners. Here are some natural sweeteners you can easily incorporate into your cooking to enhance the flavor or give it a sweet note. Some work better than others for certain dishes. Experiment with different options and use what tastes, and feels, best for you. I always recommend adjusting the type and amount to your liking. It is important, though, to remember to use all sweeteners within reason.

Look for organic options whenever possible.

Coconut Nectar

Coconut nectar is a wonderful natural sweetener. This highly nutritious sweet sap comes from tapping the stems of coconut tree blossoms and is known as the planet's most sustainable liquid sweetener. As it naturally contains a good amount of essential minerals, vitamins, and several healthy amino acids, and also has a low glycemic index, which means it won't cause your blood sugar to spike, it is a nourishing alternative to other sweeteners.

Note: Look for pure raw coconut nectar that has been minimally evaporated at a low temperature, to ensure that you enjoy the healthiest, most enzymatically alive product possible.

Medjool Dates

Medjool dates are known as the "king of dates". They originate in the Middle East and are a true delicacy. The special thing about Medjool dates is their absolutely wonderful creamy, rich, and soft texture, which develops when dates are being left to dry on the date palm before picking. Most commercially available prepacked options have been dried after gathering and just cannot live up to that very special chewiness.

Using dates has become one of my favorite ways to sweeten up my plant-based dishes. They are incredibly high in minerals, vitamins, amino acids, healthy fats, and fiber, which makes them wholesome, nutritious, and easily digestible. Eaten in moderation, dates can help support our metabolism, promote physical energy, and enhance our overall well-being. On top of that they are a wonderful treat. Medjool dates are versatile and an excellent way to create desserts. Enjoy a taste of Middle Eastern cuisine with my recipe for Date Delight (page 156).

Raw Honey

Raw honey is a wonderful natural remedy that has numerous health benefits and has been worshipped for its medicinal properties in various cultures all over the world for many centuries.

Besides being absolutely delicious in innumerable dishes, honey provides your body with a combination of wholesome nutrients that can strengthen your immune system, soothe your digestive tract, and aid in your overall well-being. It has antibacterial and anti-inflammatory properties and is also beneficial in treating wounds and skin rashes when applied externally.

Even though honey is high in sugars, it also contains essential amino acids, minerals, vitamins, and important beneficial enzymes. Due to honey's calming, soothing, and antibacterial qualities, you have a good excuse to indulge your sweet tooth without remorse when suffering from colds, viruses, or a sore throat.

Honey should be bought in its raw state from an organic, fair-trade and, whenever possible, local source. If stored in an airtight container in a dark, cool place, honey is likely to last forever. It is important to keep in mind that honey loses all its fantastic nutrients when heated up, so make sure to add honey to your dishes after cooking. I love to use it in my Golden Nut Milk (page 48) or add it to the Protect Tonic (page 68) for its healing properties.

Note: Honey should not be consumed by babies as it may contain bacteria that could harm the child. Also, because it's considered an animal product, honey isn't suitable for people following a vegan diet.

Pure Maple Syrup

North American cultures have been using maple syrup for many centuries because of its delicious sweet taste. The sap of maple trees is heated to evaporate its water, leaving the concentrated syrup, which is then filtered to remove impurities. Unfortunately, it loses some of its nutrients during the process. Among the ones left are beneficial minerals like zinc, iron, and calcium. Keep in mind, though, that maple syrup is not low on the glycemic index, yet it's a better option than refined sugar.

Maple syrup is available in a range of shades and flavors, from light golden with a delicate taste to dark amber with a robust taste. I prefer darker maple syrup, which is produced later in the harvesting season, as it has a richer and stronger flavor.

Note: When purchasing look for pure maple syrup that comes from the maple tree. A lot of commercial products are highly processed maple-flavored corn syrups.

Stevia

Stevia refers to an isolated sweet extract of the South American stevia plant that has traditionally been used as a sweetener for tea and other beverages. You can find stevia in a concentrated liquid or pulverized form. It can be a great alternative to other sweeteners because it has a glycemic index of zero. Keep in mind that stevia has a very distinctive taste and is very potent as well as much sweeter than other sweeteners. So use it in moderation, adding a small amount at a time to dishes and adjust to taste.

Look for a pure organic product and check labels, as commercially sold stevia might not be pure. For good-quality stevia you can simply make a homemade water-based extract out of dried stevia leaves. All you need is ½ cup of dried stevia leaves and 1 cup of water. Let the leaves steep for 30 to 40 minutes in simmered water, strain, and pour the liquid into a sealable glass jar. Keep refrigerated for up to 10 days.

SUPERFOODS

These days, superfoods are a hot topic and have found their way from health food stores into supermarkets. However, there is in fact no formal definition of the term "superfood." Typically, any food that is unusually dense in wonderfully nourishing nutrients—like goji berries, chlorella, or hemp seeds—can be labeled a superfood. Simply put, what makes these foods "super" is their incredible nutrient-richness that includes remarkable amounts of beneficial vitamins, minerals, antioxidants, proteins, and healthy fats.

Despite all their incredible benefits and healthful properties, superfoods won't work miracles if you don't place importance on an overall wholesome and balanced diet. You see, a handful of goji berries can do only so much. So to provide your body with the whole spectrum of nutrients it needs, it is important to integrate these dietary rock stars into a long-term healthy, plant-based diet including a lot of organically grown whole foods like greens, fruits, legumes, nuts, and seeds. I find superfoods to be a fun and delicious way to boost my well-being on many levels and make my recipes even more compelling.

The easiest way to integrate superfoods into your everyday routine is by adding them straight to your breakfast bowl or smoothie in the morning. If you prepare your lunch at home, you can simply add nuts, seeds, berries, or spices to a delicious salad or dip, and you will have a nutritious and colorful meal for the day. Start by integrating small amounts into your dishes and slowly build up your intake. Even though superfoods are amazingly yummy and incredibly nutritious, always remember to use them within reason and according to your needs and recipes.

On the following pages are some of my favorite superfoods. I like to use them as toppings for breakfast bowls or as add-ins for desserts, baked goods, and smoothies.

What's important to note: Conventionally grown superfoods are believed to include a much higher load of pesticide residues than organic products so here it is especially important to purchase the healthiest organic options possible.

Store superfoods in an airtight container in a cool, dark place for longer shelf life and to protect all their wonderful nutrients.

Bee Pollen

What many people do not know about bee pollen is that it actually has nothing to do with honey but is the food of the bee colony, which our beloved bees collect from flowers. That's why you will find its flavor to be flowery rather than honey-like, depending on the sort of pollen taken to the bee's nest. The most astounding fact about bee pollen, however, is that it's believed to be one of the most nourishing foods in the world! This powerful superfood contains almost all the nutrients the human body needs to thrive, including all the important amino acids. Not only is bee pollen superhigh in protein and healthy fatty acids, and loaded with enzymes, which help digestion, it also boosts your immune system thanks to its high amount of vitamins and trace minerals. As you can see, bee pollen is a true all-rounder!

There is one catch though: If you're allergic to pollen please make sure to first try only a tiny amount of this superfood and increase your daily intake only if you don't experience any allergic reactions.

Personally, I love to sprinkle a teaspoon of bee pollen over my daily breakfast bowl or simply blend it into my smoothies.

Raw Cacao

Great news: chocolate can be good for you! The catch: that only applies to chocolate in its raw state, not the kind with refined sugar or milk typically found on supermarket shelves.

Raw cacao beans, which are also available crushed into nibs or pulverized into powder, are an incredibly nutrient-dense food and, on top of that, superdelicious. They are an amazing source of antioxidants and have an impressive amount of minerals such as iron and magnesium. As many people today are rather deficient in magnesium, integrating raw cacao into your diet may be a delicious way to provide your body with this important nutrient.

I find raw cacao certainly gives me that special, indulgent feeling when enjoying a little treat—and for good reason: raw cacao stimulates serotonin and endorphin levels in your body. What a yummy way to improve your mood! Try not to treat yourself too much, though, as an "overdose" of cacao may lead to sleep deprivation and agitation. As with all things, use it in moderation.

You can use raw cacao in a whole range of desserts and cakes or simply as tasty decoration on sweet dishes. Two of my favorite indulgences are It's a Chocolate (page 154) and the deliciously creamy Divine Chocolate Milk (page 56).

Note: Look for organic and preferably fair-trade products.

Camu Camu Powder

Though camu camu hasn't become as popular as the açai berry yet, the fruit is thought to be as nutrient-rich as its South American neighbor. The little berry-like red fruit is native to the Peruvian rainforest and a natural vitamin C powerhouse—a real feast for the immune system. Camu camu also contains potassium, beta-carotene, and flavonoids that operate along with vitamin C as valuable antioxidants inside your system.

Since camu camu is hard to find as a fresh fruit, I recommend buying camu camu powder, which you can easily add to smoothies or juices. With its sweet and slightly sour taste, it is a great and healthy addition to many dishes.

Chia Seeds

Chia seeds have become somewhat of a superstar among superfoods. They are full of wonderful nutrients and are very versatile. Their great combination of omega-3 and omega-6 fatty acids makes chia seeds a valuable ingredient to add to your meals. The little gray (or sometimes white) seeds will keep you full a long time (due to their high protein and fiber content), enhance your endurance and strength, and also increase your energy level.

When they're mixed with a liquid ingredient, chia seeds turn into a gel that is easy to digest and can even be turned into a delicious chia pudding. Adding enough water or nut milk to dishes that contain chia seeds is therefore essential. Soaking the seeds overnight before consumption will reduce their phytic acid content and ensure that you don't miss any of their lovely benefits (for more on soaking, see page 17).

Chia seeds can be used in a variety of recipes from crackers to salads to sweeter options like pudding or breakfast bowls. They are also a great addition to baked goods, as they act like an egg substitute. Try my wonderful bread recipes (page 172 and page 174).

Chlorella

Chlorella is a freshwater green algae that has become popular for its amazing health benefits and detoxifying effects. Most of chlorella's benefits derive from its incredibly high amount of chlorophyll, which gives the algae its green color. This green pigment is called the "life blood" of plants, because it helps them convert sunrays into energy. The benefits of integrating foods rich in chlorophyll into your diet are limitless.

Chlorella's precious nutrients, including all of its amino acids, essential minerals, vitamins, and antioxidants, can vitally boost your body's blood cell production, strengthen your immune system, and support your metabolism, among other benefits. Thanks to the green powers!

If you decide to integrate pulverized chlorella in your diet, start with small amounts and build up slowly since your body needs to get used to its detoxifying effects and rich nutrients. Adding the powder to a delicious smoothie will mask its algae flavor, which can be an acquired taste. Because chlorella contains hard-to-digest cellulose walls, I recommend looking for an organic product where the cell walls have been broken down already (look at labels).

Even though chlorella is extremely nutrient-dense, it is equally important to include as many fresh, green vegetables into your diet as possible. All green vegetables are full of healthy chlorophyll; the darker the green color, the more chlorophyll is contained in the plant. My Vibrant Alkaline Green Soup recipe (page 114) is a wonderfully delicious way to feed your body with lots of green goodness. Another easy way to get your daily share of precious greens is by juicing or blending them into a smoothie. Make sure your amount of greens surpasses the amount of fruits in your drink, though, as they contain less sugar.

Goji Berries

Goji berries are called "happy berry" in Tibet, where they have been used for over two thousand years to increase longevity as well as improve health.

Goji berries are among the most nutrient-dense foods in the world and therefore almost a "must-have" in your superfood collection. They are incredibly rich in essential vitamins and trace minerals, high in beneficial antioxidants and a unique combination of amino acids. Gojis are said to have anti-aging properties, boost your immune system, enhance your mood, and promote a healthy libido, among other benefits. Gojis contain valuable amounts of vitamins A, C, and E, and even more iron than spinach, which is especially important to include into your meals when following a plant-based diet. These tiny red powerhouses are also thought to be especially beneficial for athletes, as they boost strength, endurance, and energy levels.

I find gojis to be a great addition to smoothie bowls, granola, chocolate bars and fruit and nut bars, but they can be sprinkled over green salads as well. I also like to use them for herbal teas or simply infuse my water with them, and sometimes I just enjoy them as a fruity snack. Buy only organic, pure goji berries and look for those with a medium-soft texture and dark red color.

Hemp Seeds

Even though they are closely related to the cannabis plant, hemp seeds do not cause an altered state of mind, but instead provide your body with a whole lot of essential nutrients. Among these precious nutrients are minerals like iron, magnesium, calcium and zinc, and vitamins A, B, D, and E, which all promote good overall health. The seeds also have a 3:1 ratio of omega-3 to omega-6 fatty acids, which is great for the human system. Hemp seeds can be especially beneficial for people with a very active and physical lifestyle, because the seeds contain wonderful amounts of healthy plant-based protein that includes all of the essential amino acids your body needs while being easily digestible. The high potent protein speeds up your body's regeneration processes after a workout and keeps you full for longer.

You can eat hemp seeds raw, sprouted, ground into a meal, or pulverized as protein powder. Hulled hemp seeds are softer than unhulled ones, but may not contain as much nutrients, so choose the type according to your needs and recipes. Either way, with their slightly nutty flavor they make a great addition to smoothies, juices, salads or various bowls, and plant milks (page 42).

Lucuma Powder

Lucuma is a yellow-fleshed fruit native to South America, where it has been used medicinally for centuries. On the outside, it looks a little like an avocado, and its sweet taste has been compared to mango and maple syrup.

Due to its sweetness this exotic fruit can be a wonderful alternative to your usual sweeteners. Lucuma contains a whole bunch of valuable vitamins, minerals, and antioxidants and lots of healthy fiber. Lucuma is usually dried and sold as powder, which you can use as a sweetener in numerous breakfast dishes, smoothies, or spreads, or simply sprinkle all over your desserts. Why not give it a try in ice cream, as they do in Peru? You should be able to find lucuma in many natural food stores.

Maca

Maca is a real power root and has been used by the Incas for thousands of years. It is full of healthy protein, zinc, magnesium, calcium, and iron, and greatly enhances physical performance. As the root can notably heighten energy levels, it is therefore quite popular among athletes. It is ideal for an active, busy lifestyle due to its mood balancing and stress-reducing qualities. Fun fact: maca also enjoys a good reputation as a libido booster.

The root is usually available as gelatinized or as raw maca powder. I recommend using maca in its gelatinized form, if you have a sensitive stomach and trouble digesting starch. Keep in mind that the gelatinized powder process does alter some nutrients and destroys enzyme content, but also makes it gram for gram more nutritionally dense than raw maca. Maca has a slightly sweet and malty taste so you can easily combine it with any sort of dessert or breakfast dish, including smoothies and plant-based milks, such as my super Maca Energy Oat Milk (page 54). Since it is a highly potent food, introduce it slowly into your diet.

Spirulina

Spirulina is another freshwater algae that shines with almost as many amazing health benefits as its relative chlorella. Compared to other vegetables such as carrots or spinach, spirulina has a significantly higher amount of minerals, vitamins, protein, healthy fatty acids, and antioxidants and is therefore one of the most popular superfoods on the market. Its nutrient-richness results from its main ingredient chlorophyll, a dark green pigment that is full of wonderful benefits for your body and also has a great detoxifying effect (see Chlorella, page 36).

As with chlorella, start with small amounts when introducing spirulina into your diet and slowly work yourself up. Integrating the algae in a pulverized form into delicious foods such as smoothies, dips, or pesto sauces will smoothly help to hide its distinct taste.

Turmeric

Turmeric (curcuma) is a spice that has been used in Indian traditional medicine for thousands of years for its outstanding positive effects on health. It can be found in curry (in fact, it's responsible for curry's yellow color) and various Indian remedies.

Turmeric is thought to have profound antibacterial, antiviral, antimicrobial, and anti-aging properties. Its active ingredient, curcumin, has wonderful anti-inflammatory and antioxidant effects.

You can use fresh turmeric root and grind it up yourself, or buy turmeric powder. Add it to hearty bowl dishes, curries, and soups or make it part of your salad dressings. Adding black pepper enhances the absorption of turmeric so you can fully enjoy all the wonderful benefits of the root. Sound exciting? Let me introduce you to my incredibly precious Golden Nut Milk recipe (page 48)—I just can't get enough of this flavorful goodness.

Note: Fresh turmeric will last you about one week in the fridge and several months if you place it in the freezer.

HEALTH FOOD
IS NOT ONLY
THE FUTURE
IT IS NOW

CHAPTER ONE

PLANT MILKS

ALMOND MILK

PURE, SIMPLE, AND ALKALIZING

Making your own fresh nut and seed milk is supereasy and a truly valuable and useful addition to the plant-based way of eating. I use almond milk daily!

- **7 oz/200 g raw almonds**
- **34 oz/1 liter filtered water, plus more for soaking**
- **1 teaspoon sea salt**

Place the almonds and salt in a glass or ceramic container, cover with filtered water, and soak for 8 to 12 hours. (I like to soak the almonds overnight so they are ready when I wake up in morning.) Drain the nuts, rinse them thoroughly, and remove the skins. Put them in a high-speed blender, add the filtered water, and process on high speed until deliciously creamy. Strain the milk through a nut milk bag into a container and pour into a sealable 34-ounce/1-l glass bottle.

Notes: You can keep the milk in your refrigerator for about three days. It never stays for too long in my fridge—it's just too delicious and I add the milk to many other amazing recipes.

If you desire a sweeter taste to your almond milk you can simply add 1 or 2 pitted Medjool dates, pure maple syrup, or any other sweetener of your choice to the blender.

If you'd like to try out different flavors, simply add the seeds from a fresh vanilla bean, ground cinnamon, or rose water, for example, or try your own add-ins.

You can make this milk out of any nut or seed you like, or even blend a combination. For more information on soaking times, see page 20. You can create a delicious raw hummus with the leftover nut pulp. Find the recipe on page 130.

MATCHA LATTE

MATCHA GREEN TEA POWDER + FRESH ALMOND MILK

_____

I love the taste of matcha—it reminds me of my travels to Japan and the most incredible tea ceremony I experienced there.

- ⅞ cup/200 ml fresh almond milk (page 44)
- 2 Medjool dates, pitted, (or pure maple syrup or any other sweetener)
- 1 tablespoon matcha
- 1 teaspoon organic virgin coconut oil

Combine all the ingredients in a high-speed blender and process on high speed until deliciously creamy.

Note: You can enjoy your matcha cold or hot by simply heating it up over low heat and topping it with frothy almond milk.

GOLDEN NUT MILK

THE MAGIC OF TURMERIC

This sweet and delicious ancient Ayurvedic drink provides tremendous nourishment. The health benefits of turmeric are truly extraordinary. I just love everything about this milk—the color, the taste, the scent, and, above all, the benefits. Find more information on turmeric on page 39.

- 1¼ cups/300 ml fresh almond milk (page 44), or any other plant milk you like
- 2 Medjool dates, pitted, or 1 tablespoon raw honey or maple syrup, or more to taste
- 1 tablespoon organic virgin coconut oil
- 1 teaspoon grated fresh turmeric or ground turmeric
- 1 teaspoon ground cinnamon
- pinch of grated fresh ginger or ground ginger (optional)
- small pinch of ground black pepper

Combine all the ingredients in a high-speed blender and process on high speed until wonderfully smooth. If you enjoy your Golden Nut Milk warm, heat it slowly and do not allow it to boil. If you prefer to sweeten the milk with raw honey, be sure not to heat the honey with the milk but add it afterwards to taste.

Note: Black pepper enhances the absorption of turmeric.

COCONUT MILK
SO SIMPLE. SO GOOD.

––––––––––––––––

Making your own coconut milk is so easy and the taste is so divine. This recipe always brings me back to the wonderful times I spent in Bali.

· 2 cups/160 g unsweetened shredded coconut, dried or fresh
· 4 cups/950 ml filtered water
· seeds from ½ vanilla bean
· 1–2 Medjool dates, pitted
· pinch of sea salt

Combine all the ingredients in a high-speed blender and process on high speed until deliciously creamy. Strain the milk through a nut milk bag into a container and pour into a glass bottle.

Keep refrigerated.

CASHEW MASALA MILK

CHAI SPICES + CASHEWS

_____

This special milk reminds me of my unforgettable trip through India. The second best thing about this recipe is that it fills my home with the most amazing aroma of enchanting spices. The best thing about it is, of course, the taste. Every sip touches my soul.

Cashew Milk:
• 1 cup/150 g raw cashews
• 3 cups/700 ml filtered water
• pinch of sea salt

Masala Chai:
• 2 cups/500 ml filtered water
• 2 tablespoons cardamom pods
• 1–2 cinnamon sticks
• 4–6 slices fresh ginger
• 1 star anise pod
• 2–4 whole cloves
• 2–3 black peppercorns (optional)
• pinch of ground nutmeg
• liquid sweetener (I use raw honey)

To make the cashew milk: Soak the cashews in filtered water and a pinch of salt for 4 to 6 hours. Drain the cashews and rinse well until the water runs clear. Combine the cashews and water in a high-speed blender and process on high-speed until creamy and smooth. Strain the milk through a nut milk bag into a container and pour into a glass bottle.

To make the masala chai: In a small saucepan bring the water and spices to a boil and continue simmering over low heat until the mixture is fragrant, about 20 minutes. Strain into cups through a fine-mesh sieve and add the cashew milk. Add sweetener to taste. If you prefer to sweeten your Cashew Masala Milk with raw honey, be sure not to heat it but add it afterwards to taste.

Note: If you desire a mild-flavored drink use smaller amounts of spices and the greater amounts if you like it spicy.

MACA ENERGY OAT MILK

THE MAGIC OF THE PERUVIAN ROOT

This milk is a fantastic, energizing drink. It provides a great boost to your mornings, and is equally great as an afternoon pick-me-up. Find out more about the incredible benefits of maca on page 38.

- 1⅓ cups/120 g rolled oats (gluten-free if desired),
  soaked overnight in filtered water and rinsed well
- 3 cups/700 ml filtered water
- 1 Medjool date, pitted, or more to taste (optional)
- 1 teaspoon maca powder
- ½ teaspoon lucuma powder
- seeds from ½ vanilla bean
- pinch of sea salt (I use Maldon)

Combine the oats and water in a high-speed blender and process on high speed until smooth. Strain the mixture through a nut milk bag into a bowl. Pour the milk back into the blender, add the date (if using), maca and lucuma powders, vanilla seeds, and salt and process again on high speed until creamy and silky-smooth.

DIVINE CHOCOLATE MILK

RAW CACAO + MACA + ALMOND MILK. SIMPLY DIVINE.

Did I already mention how much I love chocolate? Not only the taste of it but also its antioxidant effects. This chocolate milk is soothing for the soul and pure happiness for the mind.

- ⅞ cup/200 ml fresh almond milk (page 44), or any other nut milk you like
- 1–2 Medjool dates, pitted
- 1 heaping tablespoon raw cacao powder
- 1 teaspoon maca powder
- 1 teaspoon organic virgin coconut oil
- pinch of ground cinnamon
- pinch of ground vanilla bean powder

Combine all the ingredients in a high-speed blender and process on high speed until deliciously creamy. Enjoy hot or cold.

CHAPTER TWO

———

SMOOTHIES + BOWLS + TONICS

COCO LOVES PINEAPPLE

WHEN COCONUTS MEET PINEAPPLES—LOVE AT FIRST SIGHT!

—————————————

Hello Holiday! This incredibly refreshing drink takes you to the beach within seconds.

- ¼ ripe pineapple, cut into chunks and frozen
- ⅞ cup/200 ml coconut milk (page 50)
- 1 teaspoon chia seeds

Combine all the ingredients in a high-speed blender and process on high speed until deliciously creamy.

Note: When preparing a fresh pineapple, be sure to remove the tough core before cutting the pineapple into chunks.

CASHEW YOGURT BOWL

CAN YOU BELEVE IT? IT TASTES JUST LIKE YOGURT AND IT'S SUPERHEALTHY AS WELL!

A wonderfully delicious dairy-free yogurt option. Tasty, cultured, and so good for you!

- 2 cups/280 g raw cashews, soaked in filtered water for 8 hours and rinsed well
- ½ cup/100 ml distilled water
- 2 probiotic capsules (equal to 20 billion active cells)
- 1⅓ cups/200 g strawberries, fresh or frozen
- 1 tablespoon pure raw coconut nectar or pure maple syrup, or more if needed
- juice of ½–1 lemon
- seeds from 1 vanilla bean

Toppings:
- bee pollen
- fresh berries
- unsweetened shredded coconut
- hemp seeds
- pomegranate seeds
- granola of your choice, preferably raw
- or anything else you desire

Combine the cashews and water in a high-speed blender and process at high speed until smooth and creamy. Transfer to a sterilized glass bowl or jar, open the probiotic capsules, and add the powder to the mixture. Stir in with a wooden or plastic spoon.

Cover with a clean cloth or kitchen towel and set in a warm, dark spot for about 12 hours or overnight. The yogurt should taste tangy and sour. Transfer the yogurt to the blender, add the strawberries, coconut nectar, lemon juice, and vanilla seeds, and blend until smooth. Add more liquid sweetener or lemon juice to taste. Chill in the fridge for at least 30 minutes (longer is better) and serve with your favorite toppings.

Note: It is important to use distilled (nonchlorinated) water for this recipe, as the friendly bacteria won't survive otherwise. You can also simply use boiled water and let it cool down.

For a quicker, noncultured version, simply replace the probiotic capsules with 1 teaspoon psyllium husk powder. Blend all the ingredients at once, adding the psyllium husks, until smooth and creamy. Taste and add more liquid sweetener or lemon juice if desired. Chill in the fridge for 30 minutes. Serve with your favorite toppings.

ALOE VERA DRINK

GOOD AND HEALING

_____

This drink is refreshing; it hydrates your body and it soothes your digestive system. I like to drink a shot in the mornings.

- 3 dried plums, pitted
- ½ cup/100 ml hot filtered water
- ½ cup/100 ml pure aloe vera juice
- ½ cucumber, peeled if desired
- ½ pink grapefruit, peeled and chilled
- juice of ½ lemon
- handful fresh parsley
- ½ teaspoon camu camu powder
- pinch of fresh thyme

Soak the plums in the hot water for a minimum of 30 minutes—or better yet, overnight. Strain the plum-infused water directly into a high-speed blender, leaving the plums out, and add the aloe vera, cucumber, grapefruit, lemon juice, parsley, camu camu, and thyme. Process on high speed until smooth. Add a soaked plum if desired.

PROTECT TONIC

BOOST YOUR IMMUNE SYSTEM!

––––––––––––––––––

I like to infuse my water with a shot of these incredible powerhouse ingredients that have strong immune-boosting properties. It's a great help during cold and flu season.

- ½ cup/100 ml filtered water, or more if needed
- juice of ½ lemon
- 1–2 teaspoons raw honey
- 1 teaspoon fresh thyme
- ½–1 teaspoon bee pollen (see note)
- ½ teaspoon ground turmeric
- ½ teaspoon camu camu powder
- small piece of fresh ginger
- pinch of cayenne pepper
- pinch of freshly ground black pepper

Combine all the ingredients in a high-speed blender and process on high speed until smooth. Taste and add more honey or ginger if you like, or add more water if you desire a more liquid texture and a milder flavor. Store in the refrigerator in an airtight glass jar for up to three days. You can infuse cold or hot water with the mixture, if desired.

Note: If you're allergic to pollen, please make sure to first try only a tiny amount of bee pollen and increase your intake only if you don't experience any allergic reactions. Find out more about bee pollen on page 34.

WORKOUT SHAKES

BOOST AND RECOVER

————————————

These are great pre- and post-workout shakes to make sure you're provided with all the necessary nutrients that boost your performance and help ensure quick recovery after your workout.

Pre-Workout Energy Smoothie (drink 1 hour before your workout)

· 1–1¼ cups/250–300 ml fresh almond milk (page 44)
· ½ mango, peeled and cut into chunks, fresh or frozen
· 1 Medjool date, pitted
· 1 teaspoon organic virgin coconut oil
· 1 teaspoon organic, native and cold-pressed hemp oil
· 1 teaspoon maca powder
· pinch of ground vanilla bean powder

Post-Workout Recovery Shake (drink right after your workout)

· 1–1¼ cups/250–300 ml fresh almond milk, (page 44) hemp milk, or coconut water
· 1 ripe banana, peeled and cut into chunks, fresh or frozen
· 1 Medjool date, pitted
· 3 tablespoons/30 g raw hemp protein powder or any other plant protein powder
· pinch of sea salt (I use Maldon)
· pinch of ground vanilla bean powder
· pinch of ground cinnamon

Combine all the ingredients in a high-speed blender and process on high speed until smooth. Enjoy right away.

GREEN SMOOTHIE BOWL
I LOVE GREEN. HOW ABOUT YOU?

_____

I could add avocado to every dish all day long.
So why not also have it for breakfast in a smoothie bowl?

- 1 ripe banana, peeled, cut into chunks, and frozen
- ½ ripe avocado
- ⅞–1 cup/200–250 ml filtered water
- handful raw almonds, soaked in filtered water for 8 to 12 hours and rinsed well, skins removed (optional but preferable)
- handful spinach or kale
- handful fresh cilantro
- 1 teaspoon lucuma powder
- pinch of ground vanilla bean powder or seeds from ½ vanilla bean

Optional add-ins:
- ½ teaspoon chlorella or spirulina
- any leafy greens you like

Toppings:
- bee pollen
- unsweetened shredded coconut
- hemp seeds

Combine all the ingredients, including any add-ins (if using), in a high-speed blender and process on high speed until creamy and smooth. Pour the smoothie into a bowl and garnish with your choice of toppings.

Note: You can use 1 cup/250 ml plant milk of your choice (page 42), instead of the almonds and water.

MANGO GOODNESS
YOUR DOSE OF SUPERFOOD

This smoothie is a great start to your day. The texture, the flavor, and the health benefits are convincing indeed. Feel free to add your favorite superfoods and enjoy this nutritious goodness.

- ½ ripe mango, or more if desired, peeled, cut into chunks and frozen
- ⅔ cup/150 ml filtered water, or more if needed
- ½ cup/70 g raw cashews, soaked in filtered water for 4 to 6 hours and rinsed well (page 20)
- juice of ½ lemon
- handful fresh cilantro
- 1 teaspoon chlorella or spirulina
- 1 teaspoon bee pollen

Optional superfood add-ins:
- chia seeds
- flaxseeds
- hemp seeds
- lucuma powder
- maca powder
- 1 scoop plant protein powder

Combine all the ingredients in a high-speed blender and process on high speed until you achieve a creamy, silky, delicious texture. Enjoy right away!

Note: Find out more about superfoods on page 33.

BANANA BLISS

MAKES YOU HAPPY. MAKES ME HAPPY.

This smoothie is so deliciously creamy and sweet, almost like a dessert. And yes—it's green and kids love it! My son Sky can never get enough of it.

• ⅔ cup/150 ml fresh almond milk (page 44), or more if needed
• 1 large ripe banana, peeled, cut into chunks, and frozen
• 1 oz/30 g spinach
• handful fresh parsley
• 1–2 tablespoons almond butter (page 106)
• seeds from ½ vanilla bean

Pour the almond milk into a high-speed blender and add the banana, spinach, parsley, almond butter, and vanilla seeds. Process on high speed until creamy, silky, and delicious. Enjoy right away!

BEET AT ITS BEST

WITH APPLE + FENNEL + SPINACH + MORE

——————————————

If you are into beets and smoothies, this is the one for you.

- 1¼ cups/300 ml filtered water, or more if needed
- ½–1 small beet, peeled and cut into chunks
- 1 small apple, cored and cut into chunks
- 1 thick slice fennel, or more if desired
- handful spinach
- handful mixed berries, or more if desired, fresh or frozen
- handful fresh cilantro
- juice of ½ lemon
- 1–2 Medjool dates, pitted
- 1 or 2 slices fresh ginger
- 1 teaspoon ground cinnamon

Combine all the ingredients in a high-speed blender and process on high speed until creamy.

LAVENDER BLUEBERRY

BEAUTIFUL SHADES OF PURPLE

Lavender has been described as the soul of Provence. The blossoming fields are mesmerizing. The taste of this fragrant recipe is simply glorious.

- 1 cup/250 ml fresh almond milk (page 44)
- 1 large ripe banana, peeled, cut into chunks, and frozen
- ¾ cup/100 g blueberries, fresh or frozen
- ¼ cup/40 g raw sunflower seeds, soaked in filtered water
  for 8 hours and rinsed well (page 20)
- 1 tablespoon organic, native and cold-pressed hemp oil
- 1 teaspoon organic virgin coconut oil
- ½–1 teaspoon dried lavender flowers
- pinch of ground vanilla bean powder

Toppings:
- bee pollen
- mixed berries
- hemp seeds
- nuts and seeds (see page 20 for soaking times) or whatever your heart desires

Combine all the ingredients in a high-speed blender and process on high speed until smooth and creamy. Pour into a bowl and garnish with your choice of toppings.

BREAKFAST GOODNESS BOWL

GOOD MORNING!

———————————

I remember the first time I enjoyed a smoothie bowl—it was on a warm summer day in Los Angeles. I instantly fell in love with the idea of eating a smoothie with a spoon…. One that was beautifully decorated with an array of colorful toppings. It really inspired me—the combinations, blends, and variations of textures are endless! This smoothie is a wonderful way to start your day. Always puts a smile on my face.

• ⅞ cup/200 ml fresh almond milk (page 44), or any plant milk of your choice (page 42)
• 1 ripe mango, peeled, pitted, cut into chunks, and frozen
• 1 tablespoon organic, native and cold-pressed hemp oil
• 1 teaspoon organic virgin coconut oil
• 1 teaspoon ground turmeric
• seeds from ½ vanilla bean
• pinch of ground cinnamon
• pinch of freshly ground black pepper

Toppings:
• bee pollen
• fresh berries
• unsweetened shredded coconut
• goji berries
• granola of your choice, preferably raw
• hemp seeds
• nuts and seeds (see page 20 for soaking times)
• pomegranate seeds
• or any topping you desire

Combine all the ingredients in a high-speed blender and process on high speed until deliciously smooth. Pour the smoothie into a bowl and garnish with your choice of toppings.

PEACH LUCUMA SMOOTHIE BOWL

LUCUMA—THE GOLD OF THE INCAS

In warmer months, I love to start my day with smoothie bowls. This recipe has a delicately sweet flavor and a creamy texture.

- ⅞ cup/200 ml coconut water, coconut milk (page 50), or any other plant milk you like (page 42)
- 2 ripe peaches, pitted and cut into chunks, fresh or frozen
- ½ ripe mango or 1 banana, peeled and cut into chunks, fresh or frozen
- handful raw walnuts, soaked in filtered water for 6 to 8 hours and rinsed well (page 20)
- 1 tablespoon chia seeds, soaked overnight in 5 tablespoons filtered water
- ½ teaspoon lucuma powder
- pinch of ground vanilla bean powder

Toppings:
- bee pollen
- fresh berries
- unsweetened shredded coconut
- hemp seeds
- pomegranate seeds
- raw sunflower seeds, soaked (see page 20 for soaking times)
- any other topping you desire

Combine all the ingredients in a high-speed blender and process on high speed until smooth and creamy. Transfer to a bowl and garnish with your choice of toppings.

Note: Add a scoop of raw plant protein powder for an extra boost. I like to use raw hemp protein powder.

TAHINI OVERNIGHT OATS
WITH FRESH ALMOND MILK, TURMERIC AND BANANA + YOUR FAVORITE TOPPINGS

_____

It's a great breakfast: creamy, filling, and superdelicious!

- 1 large, ripe banana, peeled, cut into chunks, and frozen
- ⅞–1 cup/200–250 ml fresh almond milk (page 44), or more if needed
- 1 Medjool date, pitted
- 3–4 tablespoons rolled oats, soaked overnight in filtered water and rinsed well
- 1 tablespoon raw unhulled tahini
- 1 teaspoon maca powder
- ½ teaspoon ground turmeric
- pinch of ground vanilla bean powder
- pinch of ground cinnamon

Toppings:
- bee pollen
- ground cinnamon
- unsweetened shredded coconut
- goji berries
- hemp seeds
- nuts and seeds (see page 20 for soaking times)

Combine all the ingredients in a high-speed blender and process on high speed until creamy and smooth. Pour the mixture into a bowl and garnish with your choice of toppings.

Note: You can add a pinch of freshly ground black pepper to enhance the absorption of turmeric.

CHAPTER THREE

SPREADS + TOPPINGS

EATING IS LIKE MAKING LOVE.

STRAWBERRY ROSE JAM

STRAWBERRIES + ROSE WATER + CHIA SEEDS—SOUNDS GOOD, RIGHT?

This delicious jam is raw and aromatically sweet. The scent and taste take me away to strawberry fields on a warm summer day.

- 5 tablespoons chia seeds
- ⅞ cup/200 ml filtered water
- 3½ cups/500 g ripe strawberries, hulled
- 3 tablespoons pure maple syrup, or more if desired
- juice of ½ lemon
- 3–4 tablespoons rose water
- seeds from ½ vanilla bean

Mix the chia seeds with the water in a bowl and set aside for about 15 minutes, until they form a thick gel. Combine the strawberries, maple syrup, lemon juice, rose water, and vanilla seeds in a high-speed blender and process on high speed until smooth. Add the chia seeds and give it a quick blend.

Pour the jam into a 10-ounce/300-ml airtight glass container and store in the refrigerator until gelled, preferably overnight. It will keep for up to five days refrigerated.

RAW FIG JAM

FRESH FIGS + CHIA SEEDS + VANILLA BEAN

So tempting! So blissful!

- 3 tablespoons chia seeds
- ½ cup/120 ml filtered water
- 8 medium fresh figs, stems removed
- juice of 1 lemon, or more to taste
- 1 tablespoon pure maple syrup, or more to taste
- seeds from ½ vanilla bean

Mix the chia seeds with the water in a bowl and set aside for about 15 minutes, until they form a thick gel. Combine the figs, lemon juice, maple syrup, and vanilla seeds in a high-speed blender and process until smooth.

If you'd like the jam to be very creamy you can add the chia gel to the blender and blend again until smooth. If you prefer the grainy chia gel texture pour the fig mixture in a bowl and stir in the chia gel with a spoon. Place the fig jam in a 10-ounce/300-ml airtight glass jar and chill overnight in the refrigerator. It will keep for up to five days refrigerated.

APPLESAUCE

WITH BUCKWHEAT KASHA

———————————

I just had to put this recipe in this book. It's such a simple, nourishing, filling, and delicious meal that reminds me of my childhood.

Applesauce:
- 2¼ lb/1 kg apples (I like to use a mix of different apples)
- 1 tablespoon organic expeller-pressed coconut oil
- ½ teaspoon ground cinnamon
- juice of ½ lemon
- ½ teaspoon pure maple syrup, or more if desired

Kasha:
- 1¼ cups/150 g buckwheat, soaked overnight and rinsed well
- 1 teaspoon organic virgin coconut oil
- 1 teaspoon organic, native and cold-pressed hemp oil
- 1 teaspoon pure raw coconut nectar or pure maple syrup (optional)
- pinch of ground cinnamon

Toppings:
- ground cinnamon
- unsweetened shredded coconut
- hemp seeds
- fresh almond milk, warm or cold (page 44) (optional)

To make the applesauce: Peel, core, and chop the apples. In a pot, heat the coconut oil and stew the apple pieces until soft and juicy, stirring every now and then. Add the cinnamon and let the apples cool. Transfer them to a high-speed blender, add the lemon juice and maple syrup, and process on high-speed until smooth and creamy. Adjust the seasonings to taste. Store the applesauce in a 10-ounce/300-ml airtight glass container in the refrigerator for up to two days.

To make the kasha: Cook the buckwheat according to package directions. Once cooked, stir in the coconut oil, hemp oil, coconut nectar (if using), and cinnamon.

Transfer the buckwheat kasha to a bowl and generously top with applesauce. Sprinkle with cinnamon, shredded coconut, and hemp seeds. I love to pour some fresh almond milk over it as well.

MACADAMIA VANILLA RICOTTA

SIMPLY IRRESISTIBLE

_____

I celebrate this recipe! I am and probably will always be amazed by how easy it is to create a dairy flavor with nuts. This ricotta has a rich, sweet, and wonderfully creamy taste that is simply divine.

- 1¾ cups/250 g raw macadamia nuts, soaked in filtered water for 7 hours and rinsed well
- ⅞ cup/200 ml filtered water
- 4 tablespoons pure maple syrup
- 1 teaspoon maca powder
- ½ teaspoon grated lemon zest
- juice of ½ lemon
- seeds from 1 vanilla bean

Combine all the ingredients in a high-speed blender and process on high speed until deliciously creamy and smooth. Adjust seasonings and texture to taste. Serve with fresh wild figs or any other fruit you desire.

It's also super delicious with The Walnut and the Plum (page 174) or Red Velvet Brownies (page 184).

HOMEMADE COCONUT BUTTER
HEAVENLY!

_____

This is an easy way to make your own coconut butter. All you need is a little patience and you'll be rewarded with a superdelicious coconut butter, which is definitely worth it. Spread it on toasted bread or add it to smoothies, ice creams, baked goods, and desserts. Watch out—it's so good, it's a little addicting!

• 4⅓ cups/350 g unsweetened shredded coconut
• 2 tablespoons organic virgin coconut oil, if needed

Optional add-ins:
• ground cinnamon
• rose water
• vanilla bean seeds
• or any other nut or seed butter of your choice (page 106)

Process the coconut in a high-speed blender or food processor on the highest setting until a smooth butter consistency is reached. You might need to add the coconut oil to help the process if your machine doesn't have enough friction. If you desire a special flavor, you can add your favorite add-ins directly during the blending process once the smooth butter consistency is reached.

Store the coconut butter in an airtight glass jar in the refrigerator for up to one month.

Note: The consistency of coconut butter depends on the temperature; it can be solid to creamy to liquid. Refrigerated coconut butter is solid. Simply heat it in a water bath to make it smooth enough to spread. You can also give it a quick blend again to make it even creamier.

HEAVENLY CHOCOLATE BUTTER
WHEN ROASTED HAZELNUTS MEET RAW CACAO, IT'S SIMPLY DIVINE

Who would have thought making your own "Nutella" could be so easy and—most importantly—so incredibly nutritious and delicious at the same time? Enjoy...you're very welcome.

- 10½ oz/300 g raw hazelnuts
- ½ cup/120 ml fresh almond milk (page 44)
  or filtered water (if you prefer a darker chocolate taste)
- 4 tablespoons raw cacao powder
- 4 tablespoons pure maple syrup or pure raw coconut nectar, or more if needed

Optional add-ins:
- Homemade Coconut Butter, melted (page 102)
- handful crushed roasted hazelnuts (for an extra crunch)
- ground vanilla bean powder
- pinch of sea salt (I use Maldon)

Preheat the oven to 350°F/180°C. Put the hazelnuts on a baking sheet and bake until golden brown, about 15 minutes. Remove from the oven and let the hazelnuts cool. Roll them between your hands or inside a kitchen towel to remove the skins.

Place them in a food processor or high-speed blender and add the almond milk, raw cacao, and maple syrup. Process on high speed until creamy and smooth. Be patient—this might take up to 10 minutes depending on the machine you're using and the consistency you'd like to achieve. If you desire a special flavor you can add your favorite add-ins directly to the blending process.

Transfer the chocolate butter to an airtight glass container—it will make about 1¼ cups/300 g and will keep refrigerated for up to three weeks.

BASIC NUT + SEED BUTTER

THE BETTER BUTTER!

———————————

Making your own nut or seed butter is so easy and it's amazingly delicious and flavorful. The great thing about it is that you get to choose and create your own blends and textures. It just never gets boring!

• 10½ oz/300 g raw nuts and/or seeds (any kind)
• 2 tablespoons organic virgin coconut oil, melted, if needed

Optional add-ins:
• raw cacao or cacao nibs
• Homemade Coconut Butter (page 102)
• pure raw coconut nectar or pure maple syrup
• lucuma powder
• maca powder
• crushed roasted nuts and/or seeds (folded in for an extra crunch)
• sea salt
• ground vanilla bean powder
• ground cinnamon
• ground ginger
• ground cardamom
• or any other spices you desire

Preheat the oven to 350°F/180°C. Place the nuts and/or seeds on a baking sheet and bake for about 10 minutes or until golden brown. Remove from the oven and let cool. If using hazelnuts, you should remove their skins by rolling them between your hands or inside a kitchen towel.
Place the nuts and/or seeds in a food processor or high-speed blender and process on high speed until creamy and smooth. Be patient—this might take up to 10 minutes depending on the machine you're using and the consistency you'd like to achieve. You might need to add the coconut oil if there is not enough friction in your machine. If you desire a special flavor you can add your favorite add-ins during the blending process.

Transfer the butter to an airtight glass container—it will make about 1 cup/250 g and will keep refrigerated for up to three weeks.

CHAPTER FOUR

———

SOUPS

BORSCHT MY WAY

SIMPLY GOOD!

_____

This is one of my favorite soup recipes in this book. So fragrant and vibrantly beautiful. This is my version of the classic Eastern European borscht.

- 3 medium beets, peeled and chopped
- 2 medium carrots, chopped
- 6–8 plum tomatoes, quartered
- 1 small garlic clove, sliced
- 4 slices mild chile pepper
- 1 heaping tablespoon organic expeller-pressed coconut oil, melted
- leaves of 2 fresh sprigs thyme
- sea salt (I use Maldon)
- freshly ground black pepper
- 2⅛ cups/500 ml hot filtered water, or more if needed
- 1–2 tablespoons freshly squeezed lemon juice

Toppings:
- Cashew Sour Cream (page 138)
- handful fresh dill, or more if desired
- ½ teaspoon fresh shredded horseradish, or more if desired
- a few fresh mint leaves (optional)
- a few drops organic extra-virgin olive oil

Preheat the oven to 400°F/200°C. Place the beets, carrots, tomatoes, garlic and chile slices on a baking sheet and drizzle with the coconut oil, then season with thyme leaves and salt and pepper to taste. Stir and then roast, turning once or twice, until juicy and tender, about 40 minutes. Let the vegetables cool a bit and transfer three-quarters of them to a high-speed blender. Add the hot water and lemon juice and process on high speed until smooth. You may need to add more salt to taste or some more lemon juice if you prefer it more tangy.

Pour the borscht into bowls and top with the rest of the roasted veggies. Garnish with Cashew Sour Cream, dill, mint leaves (if using), and horseradish and sprinkle a few drops of olive oil over the top.

Note: I like to eat this soup with toasted Buckwheat Nut + Seed Loaf (page 172). It truly is a delicious combination.

You can enjoy the soup hot or cold—it's great both ways!

VIBRANT ALKALINE GREEN SOUP

THINK GREEN, EAT GREEN, AND FEEL AMAZING

———————————

I love everything about this soup—the color, the taste, the nutrients, and the positive effect it has on my body, my immune system, and overall health. This delicious soup is a great way to incorporate a good amount of greens into your diet, which are one of the most nutrient-dense foods available. Greens are alkalizing and will provide you with antioxidants, fiber, folate, amino acids, carotenoids, and flavonoids, among other precious nutrients. Enjoy this fantastic elixir.

- 1 tablespoon organic expeller-pressed coconut oil
- 4 oz/120 g spinach
- 3½ oz/100 g broccoli, roughly chopped
- 1 fennel bulb, finely chopped
- 2 celery stalks, chopped
- handful kale leaves, roughly chopped

- ½–1 garlic clove, sliced
- 1¼ cups/300 ml hot filtered water, or more if needed
- sea salt (I use Maldon or pink Himalayan salt)
- bunch fresh parsley
- pinch of ground cinnamon
- juice of ½ lemon

Toppings:
- daikon cress
- handful raw almonds, soaked in filtered water for 8 to 12 hours, rinsed well, and chopped
- toasted nuts and seeds

Heat the coconut oil in a large saucepan over low heat. Add the spinach, broccoli, fennel, celery, kale, and garlic and cook, stirring occasionally, until slightly soft, about 5 minutes. Add the hot water and simmer for about 5 minutes. Add salt to taste. Transfer to a high-speed blender, add the parsley, cinnamon and lemon juice, and process on high speed until smooth and creamy. If you desire a more liquid soup feel free to add more water.

Serve warm, garnished with daikon cress and almonds, or toasted nuts and seeds if you prefer.

Note: Feel free to add fresh alkalizing vegetables and leafy greens in season, such as green asparagus and chard.

FRAGRANT SWEET POTATO SOUP

A SOUP FOR THE SOUL

———————————

The flavor and vibrant color of this soup are both warming to my soul. The texture is deliciously creamy, the taste alluringly sweet. Turmeric gives it a special boost with its healing properties. I could eat this every day.

- 1 tablespoon organic expeller-pressed coconut oil
- 2 large sweet potatoes, peeled and cut into chunks
- 3 medium carrots, peeled and cut into chunks
- 3–4 slices fresh ginger
- sea salt (I use Maldon)
- 2½ cups/600 ml hot filtered water, or more if needed
- handful raw pumpkin seeds for garnish
- ⅞ cup/200 ml fresh almond milk (page 44)
- 1 teaspoon ground turmeric or grated fresh turmeric
- handful fresh cilantro, plus more for serving
- sliced fresh chile pepper (optional)
- cayenne pepper
- freshly ground black pepper
- juice of ½ lemon

Heat the coconut oil in a large saucepan over medium-high heat. Add the sweet potatoes, carrots, ginger and salt to taste and sauté, stirring occasionally, until fragrant and lightly browned. Add 1¾ cups/400 ml of the hot water and simmer until tender and the liquid is slightly reduced. While the vegetables are simmering, toast the pumpkin seeds in a skillet until lightly browned and set aside to cool.

Combine the cooked vegetables, almond milk, turmeric, and salt to taste in a high-speed blender and process on high speed until creamy and smooth. Add ⅞ cup/200 ml hot water, the cilantro, chile (if using), cayenne, and black pepper to taste and blend again. If you desire a more liquid soup feel free to add more water.

Pour the soup into bowls, sprinkle with a little lemon juice to taste, and garnish with the toasted pumpkin seeds and cilantro.

CLASSIC TOMATO SOUP
THE ABUNDANCE OF TOMATOES

I lived in Italy for some time, years ago. The joy of eating together and celebrating abundant family lunches and dinners definitely left an impression on me. This recipe is great for the whole family.

· 2 lb/900 g flavorful heirloom tomatoes, roughly chopped
· 1 cup/150 g raw cashews, soaked in filtered water for 6 hours and rinsed well
· large handful fresh basil leaves
· 3–5 slices mild red chile pepper, or more to taste
· 1 garlic clove
· ½ teaspoon fresh thyme
· cayenne pepper
· sea salt (I use Maldon)
· 1 teaspoon raw unhulled tahini (optional)
· fresh chile (optional)

Toppings:
· fresh basil
· fresh thyme
· or any other herb you desire
· organic extra-virgin olive oil

Combine all the ingredients in a high-speed blender and process on high speed until smooth and creamy. You can either enjoy the soup warm by heating it up in a pot or drink it cold straight out of the blender. If you're using a Vitamix you can blend it on high speed until warm. Pour the soup into bowls and garnish with herbs and sprinkle with olive oil.

Notes: If you prefer a soup with more heartiness and flavor, you can roast your tomatoes and garlic before blending them with the rest of the ingredients. Simply preheat the oven to 400°F/200°C, place the chopped tomatoes and the garlic clove on a large baking sheet, drizzle with some melted organic expeller-pressed coconut oil, sprinkle with salt, and roast for 10 to 15 minutes. Let cool slightly before blending.

Serve the soup with these superdelicious options:
legumes (page 21), whole grains (page 23), Buckwheat Nut + Seed Loaf (page 172), Cashew Basil Parsley Dip (page 142), Cashew Sour Cream (page 138), Pea Pistachio Party (page 126) , The Walnut and the Plum (page 174)

AVOCADO GAZPACHO

AVOCADO LOVE

I could dedicate a whole chapter to avocados. Their smooth, creamy texture and special flavor had me at "hello." I celebrate this fantastic gift from nature with this recipe.

- 1½ perfectly ripe large avocados, halved, pitted, and peeled
- 1½ large English cucumbers (about 10 oz/300 g), peeled and chilled
- 1¾ cups/400 ml cold filtered water
- juice of 1 lemon or lime, less or more if needed
- small handful fresh cilantro
- sea salt (I use Maldon)
- a few fresh mint leaves
- 1 teaspoon organic virgin coconut oil
- ½ garlic clove, minced (optional)
- ½ teaspoon finely chopped shallot (optional)
- slices of fresh chile pepper (optional)

Toppings:
- minced fresh chives
- chopped fresh cilantro
- sliced or chopped cucumber
- chopped fresh mint leaves
- roasted black sesame seeds

Combine all the ingredients in a high-speed blender and process on high speed until smooth. Do not overblend, as the avocado might become too warm and turn bitter. Adjust the seasonings to taste and chill before serving. Garnish with your choice of toppings.

CHAPTER FIVE

DIPS + DRESSINGS

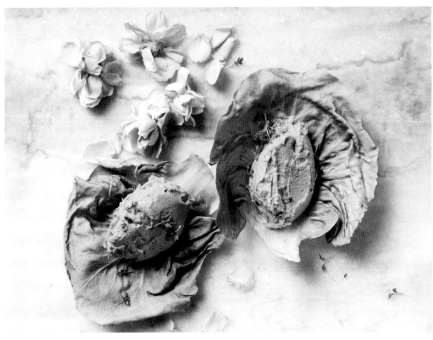

PEA PISTACHIO PARTY

IT'S A HUMMUS. IT'S SO GOOD!

_____

I. Love. Peas.

- 2 cups/300 g peas, freshly shelled or frozen
- 3 tablespoons + 1 teaspoon/50 ml filtered water
- ¼ cup/60 ml organic extra-virgin olive oil, plus more for drizzling
- juice of 1 lemon, or more to taste
- 1 tablespoon raw unhulled tahini
- ½ garlic clove (optional)
- pinch of sea salt (I use Maldon)
- large bunch fresh cilantro
- pinch of cayenne pepper
- ½ cup/60 g pistachios, chopped

Steam the peas and set aside to cool. Combine the peas, water, oil, lemon juice, tahini, garlic (if using), salt, and most of the cilantro in a high-speed blender and process on high speed until creamy. Scrape down the sides if needed. Add the cayenne, then taste and adjust the flavor and texture to your liking; for instance, add more lemon juice if you'd like it tangier or more water for a thinner consistency. Spoon the pea hummus into your favorite dish, garnish with chopped pistachios and cilantro, and drizzle some olive oil over the top. Super delicious!

Note: You can replace the peas with chickpeas or any other legume you like (page 21). Have fun with it, experiment, and always adjust to taste!

MINT CHUTNEY

WITH PARSLEY, SHREDDED COCONUT, FRESH GINGER + MORE

My unforgettable trip to India inspired me to create this recipe. This is my version of mint chutney that is refreshingly flavorful.

- ⅔ cup/150 ml fresh almond milk, or more if needed (page 44)
- ½ cup/70 g raw almonds, soaked in filtered water for 8 to 12 hours and rinsed well
- 6 tablespoons organic extra-virgin olive oil
- large bunch fresh parsley
- large handful fresh mint
- juice of 1½ limes
- 1 tablespoon unsweetened shredded coconut
- ¼ garlic clove, minced, or more to taste
- 2 slices fresh ginger
- 2 slices fresh chile pepper, or more to taste
- pinch of ground cumin
- sea salt (I use Maldon)

Combine all the ingredients in a food processor or high-speed blender. Give it a quick blend if you like the mint chutney chunky or process longer for a smooth consistency. If using a blender you might want to use your tamper to push ingredients into the blades.

Serve with salad, veggies, quinoa (page 24), rice or any other whole grain and legume you like.

ALMOND HUMMUS

ALMONDS + TAHINI + LEMON + CUMIN

_____

This dish reminds me of my many travels to Tel Aviv. Every trip to that amazing city was all about tasting the best hummus in town. It literally became a hunt. I remember having to bring back batches for family and friends. This is my version; I put a twist on the recipe and replaced the chickpeas with raw almond pulp.

- 4.6 oz/130 g almond pulp,
  left over from making fresh almond milk (page 44), more if desired
- ⅓ cup/80 ml filtered water, more if needed
- 2.5 oz/70 g raw unhulled tahini (for homemade tahini see recipe page 106), more if desired
- juice of 1 large lemon, or more to taste
- 1 garlic clove, crushed
- ½–1 teaspoon ground cumin
- sea salt (I use Maldon)
- cayenne pepper

For serving:
- 1–2 teaspoons organic extra-virgin olive oil
- black sesame seeds (optional)
- cayenne pepper

Combine all the ingredients, including cumin, salt, and cayenne to taste, in a high-speed blender or food processor and process until creamy. Add more lemon juice, salt, cayenne or cumin if you desire. If you want a thicker hummus add more almond pulp. Place the hummus in a bowl and drizzle the olive oil over it, then sprinkle with sesame seeds (if desired), and cayenne.

CREAMY FLAVORFUL NUT SAUCE

WITH ROASTED EGGPLANT

_____

I love everything about nuts! I do! And I find myself using them for almost every recipe—blending them in, using them as toppings for sweet and savory dishes. I am going for it. Can't help it—they're just too good and versatile.

Nut Sauce:
- 9 tablespoons/140 ml filtered water, or more if needed
- 2 tablespoons nut butter, any kind you like (page 106)
- juice of ½ lime
- 1½ teaspoons chickpea miso, or any miso you like
- 3–4 slices fresh chile pepper

- 1 garlic clove
- pinch of sea salt (optional; I use Maldon)
- cayenne pepper
- handful fresh cilantro

Eggplants:
- 3 large eggplants
- 3 tablespoons organic expeller-pressed coconut oil, melted
- pinch of sea salt
- freshly ground pepper

For serving:
- fresh cilantro, chopped
- nuts and seeds
- slices of fresh chile pepper (optional)

To make the nut sauce: Combine the water, nut butter, lime juice, miso, chile pepper, garlic, salt, and cayenne to taste in a high-speed blender and process on high speed until smooth and creamy. Adjust the seasonings to taste and add more water if you desire a more liquid consistency. Add the cilantro and give it another quick blend.

To make the eggplants: Preheat the oven to 350°F/180°C. Trim the stems off the eggplants and cut them in half lengthwise. With a knife, score diagonal lines deep into the flesh of each half but not through the skin, in a diamond pattern. Place the eggplant halves on a baking sheet, cut side up, and brush generously with coconut oil. Repeat until all of the oil has been absorbed by the flesh and sprinkle with salt and pepper. Roast for 30 to 40 minutes, or until the eggplants are completely soft and flavorful.

To serve: Spoon the nut sauce generously over the eggplant halves and sprinkle with cilantro, nuts and seeds, and fresh chile if you desire.

Note: You can also serve the sauce with quinoa (page 24), lentils (page 22), steamed or roasted vegetables, or even use it as a salad dressing. Feel free to experiment.

SUNFLOWER-LEMON DRESSING

THE PERFECT REFRESHING ADDITION TO YOUR SALADS

_____

This dressing is so easy and quick to make. If you love fresh salads the way I do, this recipe is definitely for you!

- ½ cup/120 ml filtered water, or more if needed
- ¾ cup/100 g raw hulled sunflower seeds, soaked for 8 hours in filtered water and rinsed well
- large bunch fresh parsley
- 2 tablespoons organic extra-virgin olive oil
- juice of ½ to 1 lemon
- pinch of cayenne pepper
- ¼ garlic clove (optional)
- sea salt (I use Maldon)

Combine all the ingredients, including salt to taste, in a high-speed blender and process on high speed until smooth and creamy, adding water as needed. Adjust according to your taste and preferred consistency.

SPICY TAHINI SAUCE

WITH PAN-FRIED BABY ARTICHOKES

_____

I cannot get enough of this tahini.

Tahini Sauce:
- ⅞ cup/200 ml filtered water
- 3 tablespoons raw unhulled tahini (for homemade tahini see recipe page 106)
- juice of 2 lemons
- ½ garlic clove (optional)
- pinch of ground cumin
- sea salt (I use Maldon)
- cayenne pepper

Pan-Fried Baby Artichokes:
- 12 baby artichokes
- juice of ½ lemon
- sea salt
- organic expeller-pressed coconut oil for greasing the pan
- 1 garlic clove, lightly crushed
- 1 teaspoon fresh thyme

To make the tahini sauce: Combine all the ingredients, including salt and cayenne to taste, in a high-speed blender and process on high speed until smooth and creamy. Adjust the seasonings and consistency to taste.

To make the fried baby artichokes: Snap off the hard outer leaves of the artichokes to expose the tender, pale green leaves. With a sharp knife, cut off the stem and the top quarter of each artichoke. Now cut the artichokes in half.

Bring water to a boil in a large pot. Add the lemon juice and salt to taste and boil the artichokes for about 2 minutes. Drain the artichokes.

Heat a large skillet, grease with coconut oil and fry the artichokes with the garlic until golden brown and crispy on the outside and tender on the inside. Add the thyme and season with salt to taste.

Note: You can also enjoy the tahini sauce with any whole grains (page 23) you like, with vegetables, and with salads.

CASHEW SOUR CREAM
WITH ROASTED SWEET POTATO FRIES

_____

A plant-based sour cream. YES! It's creamy, it's rich, it's tangy, it's perfect!

Sour Cream:
- 2 cups/300 g raw cashews, soaked in filtered water for 4 to 6 hours and rinsed well
- ⅔ cup/150 ml filtered water, or more if needed
- juice of 2 lemons, or more if desired
- sea salt (I use Maldon)

Fries:
- 2 large sweet potatoes, unpeeled, scrubbed clean
- 2 tablespoons organic expeller-pressed coconut oil, melted
- sea salt (I use Maldon)
- cayenne pepper
- 1 teaspoon fresh thyme

Optional toppings:
- fresh garlic, minced
- fresh oregano
- fresh rosemary
- freshly ground black pepper
- black sesame seeds

To make the sour cream: Combine all the ingredients, including salt to taste, in a high-speed blender and process on high speed until smooth and creamy. Adjust the flavor and texture to your liking by adding more lemon juice, salt, or water if desired.

To make the fries: Preheat the oven to 350°F/180°C. Cut each potato lengthwise into even sticks and place in a bowl. Drizzle with the coconut oil and toss with your hands to make sure they are well coated. Place the potato sticks in a single layer on a baking sheet and sprinkle with salt, cayenne and fresh thyme, or any other topping you desire. Bake until tender and golden brown and crispy on the edges, about 20 minutes. Serve with the cashew sour cream.

Note: Feel free to experiment and try different seasonings for your sweet potato fries.

CILANTRO-COCONUT PESTO

THE COMBINATION!

_____

Cilantro and coconut always remind me of Thai cuisine and bring back fond holiday memories. I adore this recipe and hope you do, too.

- 4 bunches fresh cilantro
- 1⅓ cups/200 g raw cashews, soaked in filtered water for 4 to 6 hours and rinsed well, or raw almonds, soaked in filtered water for 8 to 12 hours and rinsed well
- juice of 1 lemon, or more to taste
- 2 tablespoons organic virgin coconut oil
- 2 tablespoons organic extra-virgin olive oil
- 1 teaspoon unsweetened shredded coconut
- 2–3 slices fresh chile pepper (optional)
- sea salt (I use Maldon)
- pinch of cayenne pepper

Combine all the ingredients in a high-speed blender or a food processor and process until smooth. If you prefer your pesto chunky use the pulse function. Add more lemon juice, salt, or chile to taste.

Note: Of course you can replace the cashews with walnuts, macadamia nuts, or any nuts you like. See page 20 for appropriate soaking times. Enjoy this dip with raw veggie sticks and salads, a bowl of rice with steamed vegetables, or just spread on some bread (page 172).

CASHEW BASIL PARSLEY DIP

WITH LEMON, TOMATOES, AND CAYENNE

If you love cashews, this recipe is for you! It's creamy, filling, delicious, smooth, sweet, yet hearty and tangy at the same time.

- ⅞ cup/120 g raw cashews, soaked in filtered water for about 4 hours and rinsed well
- 6–8 cherry tomatoes
- juice of 1 lemon
- handful fresh basil leaves, or more to taste
- handful fresh parsley, or more to taste
- pinch of cayenne pepper
- sea salt (I use Maldon)
- slices of fresh chile pepper (optional)

Combine all the ingredients, including salt and chile pepper (if using) to taste, in a high-speed blender and process on high speed until creamy and smooth.

Note: Enjoy this dip with veggies and salads or just spread it on some bread (page 172).

CASHEW CURRY CREAM

WITH ROASTED TURMERIC CAULIFLOWER

This is one of my favorite blends—it's so delicious and nourishing. I call it the happy meal for the soul. Maybe I'm attached to it because it brings back all those incredible memories and insights from my travel to India—the colors, the beauty, and extreme aromas of a country that is truly something else. Words cannot really describe it... but the taste of this Cashew Curry Cream can.

Cream:
- 1⅓ cups/200 g raw cashews, soaked in filtered water for 4 to 6 hours and rinsed well
- 1¾ cups plus 3 tablespoons/220 ml fresh almond milk (page 44) or filtered water
- 2 teaspoons mild or hot curry powder (I use mild)
- 2 slices fresh ginger
- ½ garlic clove (optional)
- pinch of ground cumin
- pinch of ground cinnamon
- pinch of cayenne pepper
- sea salt (I use Maldon)
- handful fresh cilantro, finely chopped
- ½ sweet small onion, minced (optional)

Cauliflower:
- 1 medium to large head cauliflower
- 2 tablespoons expeller-pressed coconut oil, melted
- 1 teaspoon ground turmeric
- sea salt

Toppings:
- handful fresh cilantro, chopped
- handful raisins or chopped Medjool dates

To make the cream: Combine the cashews, almond milk, curry powder, ginger, garlic, cumin, cinnamon, cayenne, and salt to taste in a high-speed blender and process on high speed until smooth and creamy. Stir in the cilantro and onion (if using) and adjust the seasonings to taste.

To make the cauliflower: Preheat the oven to 350°F/180°C. Line a baking sheet with parchment paper. Cut the cauliflower lengthwise in thick slices and lay them in a single layer on the prepared baking sheet. Sprinkle with the coconut oil, turmeric, and salt to taste and roast for about 30 minutes, until tender and golden.

To serve: Gently heat the cashew curry cream in a saucepan over very low heat (or enjoy it cold if you prefer). Generously drizzle the cauliflower with the cashew curry cream, sprinkle with raisins, and garnish with cilantro.

Note: This sauce tastes amazing with beluga or le Puy lentils (page 22). Of course you can serve it with any other legumes or vegetables as well. Feel free to experiment and add variety to your meals.

BACK TO THE ROOTS

CHREIN MY WAY: BEET + HORSERADISH + CASHEWS

――――――――――

This Jewish relish was inspired by my dad's love for chrein (horseradish) and gefilte fish. I dropped the gefilte and gave it my own twist. I love to eat it with roasted veggies and a wild herb and baby leaf salad. But of course you can feel free to enjoy it with whatever you fancy. It's simply delicious and dear to my heart!

- 1¾ cups/250 g raw cashews, soaked in filtered water for 4 to 6 hours and rinsed well
- ¾ cup/180 ml filtered water, or more if needed
- 1 large beet
- 2 oz/50 g fresh horseradish root, peeled, or more to taste
- juice of 1 lemon
- sea salt (I use Maldon)

Combine all the ingredients, including salt to taste, in a high-speed blender and process on high speed until smooth and creamy. Add more salt and horseradish if you desire a stronger flavor and process again.

Note: Serve with roasted root vegetables, whole grains, salad, or just on a slice of Buckwheat Nut + Seed Loaf (page 172).

147

CHAPTER SIX

———

SWEETS

IT'S A CHOCOLATE

AND A MELT-IN-YOUR-MOUTH EXPERIENCE

_____

No need to say more. Taste it for yourself.

• 9 oz/250 g raw cold-pressed cacao butter
• 1⅔ cups/150 g raw cacao powder
• ½–⅔ cup/100–150 ml pure raw coconut nectar, pure maple syrup,
  or any liquid sweetener (page 31)
• 1 teaspoon ground vanilla bean powder or seeds from 1 vanilla bean
• pinch of sea salt (I use Maldon)

Toppings:
• roasted almonds with almond butter (page 106)
• unsweetened shredded coconut
• goji berries and hemp seeds
• dried lavender flowers
• matcha powder
• roasted pumpkin seeds
• or any other combinations you desire

Before making the chocolate note that it is very important that all the bowls and utensils you use are completely dry.

Line a baking sheet with parchment paper or use a nonstick baking sheet. Bring some water to simmer in a saucepan over low heat. Place the cacao butter in a heatproof bowl and set it on the saucepan over the simmering water. Heat gently, stirring occasionally, until melted.

In a second bowl, combine the cacao powder, coconut nectar, vanilla powder, and salt. Add the melted cacao butter and whisk all the ingredients until smooth. Add more sweetener to taste. Pour immediately onto the baking sheet, smooth evenly, and sprinkle with your choice of toppings before the chocolate is solid.

Place in the refrigerator for about 30 minutes to firm and for another 10 minutes in the freezer. Break or cut the chocolate into pieces and transfer to an airtight container. Keep the chocolate refrigerated.

Note: Using a sweetener that wonderfully complements the chocolate flavor and experience is a matter of personal taste. So feel free to experiment with the different sweeteners recommended on page 30 according to what feels best for you. As with all sweeteners, use within reason.

DATE DELIGHT
A TASTE OF MIDDLE EASTERN CUISINE

_____

I am so into Medjool dates! Their rich flavor is exquisite, their sweet taste and juicy flesh truly alluring. I totally understand why they are called the king of dates.

- 20 large Medjool dates, pitted
- 100 ml fresh almond milk (page 44), or any other plant milk or water, or more if needed
- 2 tablespoons raw unhulled almond butter, or any nut or seed butter you desire (page 106)
- juice of ½ lemon, or more if desired
- seeds from 1 vanilla bean
- pinch of sea salt (I use Maldon)

Toppings:
- apple or pear slices
- bee pollen
- unsweetened shredded coconut
- fresh figs, quartered
- hemp seeds
- fresh raspberries
- toasted pistachios

Place the dates in a small bowl, press them down, and cover with the almond milk. Soak for at least 30 minutes. Add the dates and almond milk to a high-speed blender, add all the other ingredients, and process on high speed until smooth and creamy. Use a tamper to push the ingredients into the blades. Place in the refrigerator for about 30 minutes before serving with your favorite toppings.

Note: Store in an airtight glass container in the fridge for up to three days. Date Delight also makes a wonderful spread.

RAW CHOCOLATE SEMIFREDDO

WITH RAW CACAO, LUCUMA POWDER, DATES, AND NUTS

_____

This is perfect if you desire something chocolaty, nutty, ice cream-y, and chocolate mousse-y. This is my version of a semifreddo, the texture somewhere between a luscious frozen chocolate mousse and gelato.

- 2¾ cups/400 g raw cashews, soaked in filtered water for about 6 hours and rinsed well
- ⅞ cup/200 ml filtered water
- 4 tablespoons raw cacao powder
- 5 Medjool dates, pitted
- juice of 1 lemon
- 2 tablespoons organic virgin coconut oil
- 2 tablespoons pure maple syrup or pure raw coconut nectar, or more if needed
- 2 teaspoons lucuma powder
- 1 teaspoon maca powder
- seeds from 1 vanilla bean
- pinch of sea salt (I use Maldon)
- ⅔ cup/65 g raw walnuts and ⅔ cup/95 g raw almonds,
  soaked in filtered water overnight and rinsed well

Combine the cashews, water, cacao powder, dates, lemon juice, coconut oil, maple syrup, lucuma powder, maca powder, vanilla seeds, and salt in a high-speed blender and process on high speed until smooth and creamy. The mixture should be thick; if it's too watery, add more cashews or dates. If the mixture is too thick, like heavy cream, add a little more water. Taste and add more liquid sweetener or lemon juice if needed. Add the walnuts and almonds and give it a quick blend or pulse a few times for crunchy bits. Spoon the mixture evenly into the cups of a 12-cup silicone muffin form. Put in the freezer for at least 4 to 6 hours. Remove the semifreddo from the freezer and unmold it about 20 minutes before serving.

MATCHA ICE CREAM

FOR ALL MATCHA AND ICE CREAM LOVERS: THIS ONE IS TRULY TEMPTING!

Tokyo, Japan. I was on an incredibly fascinating food journey. Matcha always reminds me of that trip. Besides being served as tea, matcha seemed to be everywhere and in everything—cookies, ice cream, noodles, bread, cakes, crepes, fudge, granola, chocolate, lemonade… I could go on and on. If you dream it you can make it with matcha.

- 1¾ cups/250 g raw cashews, soaked in filtered water for 4 to 6 hours and rinsed well
- ½ cup/100 ml fresh almond milk (page 44)
- 5 bananas, peeled, cut into chunks, and frozen
- seeds from 1 vanilla bean
- 1–2 tablespoons matcha powder
- 1–2 teaspoons pure maple syrup (optional)

Combine all the ingredients in a high-speed blender and process on high speed until completely smooth and creamy. Use the tamper to push the ingredients into the blades. Pour the mixture into a glass or metal container (I use a baking dish). Cover with plastic wrap or a lid and place in the freezer. Allow the ice cream to set for at least 6 hours. Let thaw for about 20 minutes before serving.

Note: You can make delicious matcha ice cream sandwiches with Toasted Pistachio Cookies (page 182).

Once the ice cream is thawed and it's easy to scoop, place a generous scoop on top of a cookie and gently press down with a spatula. Place another cookie on top, press to set, and enjoy! You can freeze your matcha ice cream sandwiches in an airtight glass container for later. They will keep for about one week in the freezer.

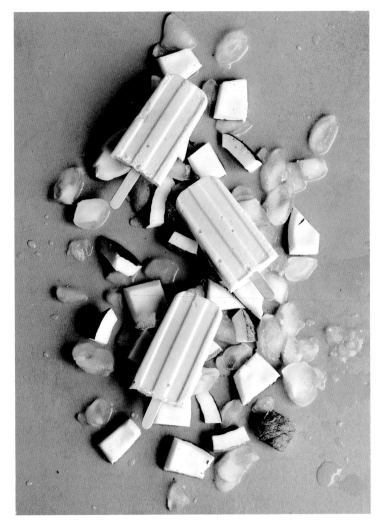

COCONUT-PINEAPPLE
ICE POPS

THE TASTE OF SUMMER

———————————

Each bite brings you closer to the beach.

- 2½ cups/400 g fresh, ripe, sweet pineapple chunks, chilled
- 1¼ cups/180 g raw cashews, soaked in filtered water for 4 to 6 hours and rinsed well
- 7 tablespoons coconut puree or coconut manna, melted
- ½ cup/100 ml fresh almond milk (page 44) or coconut milk (page 50)
- 1–2 tablespoons pure raw coconut nectar, or more if needed
- juice of ½ lemon
- seeds from ½ vanilla bean
- ⅔ cup/50 g unsweetened shredded coconut

Combine the pineapple, cashews, coconut puree, almond milk, lemon juice, coconut nectar, and vanilla seeds in a high-speed blender and process on high speed until smooth and creamy. Use a tamper to push everything into the blades. Add the shredded coconut and pulse a few times. Adjust the flavor and sweetness to your taste.

Pour the mixture into ice pop molds (about eight, depending on their size). Insert the ice pop sticks and freeze until firm, at least 6 hours. Let them thaw for about 5 minutes before serving. You can keep the ice pops in the freezer for later. They will keep for about five days, but I think they are best when enjoyed right away.

Note: When preparing a fresh pineapple, be sure to remove the tough core before cutting the pineapple into chunks.

RAW CHEESECAKE

WOW

———————————

I lived in NYC in my 20s—it was so exciting and alive. This city definitely has a special pace, dynamism, and a beat of its own. I dedicate this recipe to New York City.

Crust:
- ⅞ cup/100 g raw walnuts, soaked in filtered water for 7 hours and rinsed well
- ⅓ cup/50 g raw almonds, soaked in filtered water for 8 to 12 hours and rinsed well
- 11 large Medjool dates, pitted
- pinch of ground cinnamon

Filling:
- 2½ cups/370 g raw cashews, soaked in filtered water for 4 to 6 hours and rinsed well
- ¾ cup/180 ml fresh almond milk (page 44)
- ¼ cup/50 ml pure maple syrup or coconut nectar, more or less to taste
- 2 tablespoons organic expeller-pressed coconut oil
- juice of 2 lemons

- seeds from 1 vanilla bean
- pinch of sea salt (I use Maldon)

Optional flavor add-ins:
- raw almond butter
- blueberries or raspberries
- unsweetened shredded coconut
- lavender
- toasted pistachios
- rose water
- or any other flavor you like

To make the crust: Put the walnuts and almonds in a food processor or high-speed blender and process until chunky. Remove and set aside. Now add the dates to the food processor or blender and process until minced. Add the ground nuts and cinnamon and process until a sticky mixture forms.

Divide the crust mixture into six even portions and press one into each cup of a six-cup silicone muffin form. You can use the bottom of a glass to really press the crust into the cups. Place in the freezer to firm up for at least 30 minutes.

To make the filling: Combine all the ingredients in a high-speed blender and process on high speed until silky-smooth. Taste and add more sweetener or lemon juice if needed. Spoon the filling evenly into the muffin cups. You can either add any flavor add-ins during the blending process or stir them into the cheesecake mixture after spooning it into the cups.

Freeze for 4 to 6 hours. Remove the cheesecakes from the freezer and unmold them about 20 minutes before serving.

COCONUT ROSE WATER BITES
I'M IN HEAVEN!

_____

Coconut and all the incredible ingredients derived from it are nature's gift to us. This food is so unique, so amazing, versatile, and nourishing—I am simply overwhelmed.

- 2½ cups/200 g unsweetened shredded coconut
- 3½ tablespoons coconut puree or coconut manna, melted
- 2 tablespoons coconut flour
- 2–3 tablespoons pure raw coconut nectar or pure maple syrup
- 2–3 tablespoons organic virgin coconut oil
- 2–3 tablespoons rose water
- seeds from 1 vanilla bean
- pinch of sea salt (I use Maldon)

Toppings:
- unsweetened shredded coconut
- hemp seeds
- crushed raw pistachios

Place all ingredients in a high-speed blender or food processor and process on high speed until you achieve a dough consistency. Use your tamper to push everything into the blades. Place your choice of toppings in a shallow dish. Using a small ice cream scoop, form the mixture into balls and roll them in the topping. Place the balls on a parchment-lined tray or baking sheet and set them in the refrigerator until firm. Store in an airtight glass container in the refrigerator for up to three days.

CHAPTER SEVEN

———

BREADS + BATTERS

BUCKWHEAT NUT + SEED LOAF

A PERFECTLY NUTTY BITE

Baking gluten-free bread seems to be a real art. After experimenting a few times and eating my way through a few less-than-perfect loaves, this bread was born.

- ¼ cup chia seeds
- 2⅛ cups/500 ml filtered water
- 1 cup/100 g rolled oats (gluten-free if desired)
- 1 cup/100 g ground flaxseeds
- ⅞ cup/100 g buckwheat flour
- 2 tablespoons organic expeller-pressed coconut oil
- 1 tablespoon maple syrup
- 1 tablespoon baking soda
- ½ teaspoon sea salt (I use Maldon)
- ¾ cup/100 g raw pumpkin seeds, hulled
- ⅔ cup/100 g raw sunflower seeds, hulled
- ⅓ cup/50 g raw sesame seeds, unhulled
- ¼ cup/30 g raw hazelnuts

Mix the chia seeds with ⅞ cup/200 ml of the water in a bowl and set aside for about 15 minutes until they form a thick gel. Line a 9 by 5-inch/23 by 12-cm loaf pan with parchment paper. Meanwhile, combine the remaining 1¼ cups/300 ml water, oats, flaxseeds, buckwheat flour, coconut oil, maple syrup, baking soda, and sea salt in a high-speed blender and blend on high speed until smooth. Add the chia gel and blend again until you have a thick batter. Pour the mixture into a bowl, add the pumpkin seeds, sunflower seeds, sesame seeds, and hazelnuts, and stir until well combined. Pour the batter into the loaf pan and spread it evenly. Cover with a kitchen towel and set aside at room temperature for about 2½ hours.

About 30 minutes before baking, preheat the oven to 400°F/200°C. Bake the loaf for 1 hour or until a toothpick inserted in the center comes out clean. Let it cool completely at room temperature before slicing, as this is a delicate bread.

Notes: You can store the bread in an airtight container or kitchen towel in the fridge for about five days. Or slice and freeze it, and toast it whenever you fancy a nutty bite.

I enjoy this bread toasted and simply topped with avocado, It's also good with spreads (page 90), dips (page 124), and soups (page 110).

THE WALNUT AND THE PLUM
A BREAD FULL OF FLAVOR AND GOODNESS

I discovered teff flour only a while ago. It has a mild and nutty flavor that goes very well with other flours, such as buckwheat. Not only is teff gluten-free, but this Ethiopian/Eritrean grain also has great nutritional value (page 28). This recipe is so flavorful. The bread is soft and sticky inside and crusty outside–to me, the perfect kind of bread.

- Organic expeller-pressed coconut oil, for greasing the cake pan
- 2 tablespoons chia seeds
- 7 tablespoons/100 ml filtered water (for soaking the chia seeds), plus hot filtered water (for soaking the dried plums), plus 3 cups/700 ml warm filtered water (for the dough)
- 3 oz/80 g pitted dried plums (prunes)
- 1½ cups/250 g teff flour, plus more to sprinkle on the bread
- 1 cup/100 g rolled oats (gluten-free if desired)
- 7 tablespoons/50 g buckwheat flour
- 2 teaspoons sea salt, plus more to sprinkle on the bread (I use Maldon)
- 1 teaspoon baking soda
- ⅔ cup/60 g raw walnuts
- 2 tablespoons fresh lemon juice
- 1 teaspoon fresh thyme

Preheat the oven to 350°F/180°C and grease a 6-inch/15-cm cake pan with coconut oil.

Mix the chia seeds with 7 tablespoons/100 ml water in a bowl and set aside for about 15 minutes until they form a thick gel. In a separate bowl, soak the dried plums in hot water until soft, then drain. Meanwhile combine the teff flour, oats, buckwheat flour, sea salt, and baking soda in a large bowl.

Pour 3 cups/700 ml warm water into a high-speed blender, add the flour mix, and blend on low speed until combined. Add the chia seeds and blend on slow speed again. The mixture will be quite sticky. Return the mixture to the bowl and add the dried plums, walnuts, lemon juice, and thyme. Mix well with a large spoon or your hands—the batter is very sticky and moist, but don't worry, that's how it should be. Place the batter immediately in the pan and spread it evenly. Sprinkle with a little teff flour and sea salt and bake for 1 hour to 1 hour 10 minutes. The bread should be crusty outside and moist inside. Let it cool completely before cutting.

Note: Enjoy this bread with spreads (page 90), dips (page 124), and soups (page 110), or simply on its own. It's so good!

CRACKER TIME

THREE WAYS

A cracker always comes in handy—especially when you have kids and need a quick snack or something nice to nibble on. These crackers are also great for travels, a good alternative to trail mixes. And they are superdelicious with spreads (page 90), dips (page 124), and soups (page 110).

- 1⅔ cups/200 g buckwheat flour
- 1 cup/250 ml fresh almond milk (page 44)
- ½ cup/50 g rolled oats (gluten-free if desired)
- 1 heaped tablespoon organic expeller-pressed coconut oil
- pinch of sea salt (I use Maldon)

Preheat the oven to 350°F/180°C. Line a baking sheet with parchment paper. Combine all the ingredients in a high-speed blender and blend until smooth. Spread the batter evenly on the baking sheet . Bake for 20 to 30 minutes, depending on how thick your mixture is. The thinner the batter the crispier the crackers will be. Let cool completely before breaking into pieces.

Variations:

Add 3 tablespoons/15 g unsweetened shredded coconut and a pinch of ground vanilla bean powder to the high-speed blender with the other ingredients. Sprinkle the batter with a handful hemp hearts and sunflower seeds before baking.

Sprinkle the batter with fresh thyme and rosemary to your liking, cayenne pepper, and sea salt to taste.

Sprinkle the batter with a handful black sesame seeds and crumbled nori.

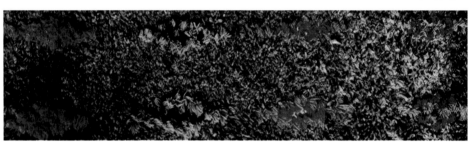

BANANA BREAD
Y.U.M.M.Y.

———————————

I was never a huge fan of baking, I have to admit. I have the utmost respect for people who have a talent for baking, as it truly requires skills—everything you do and all the ingredients you use have to be in the right combination and proportion. When my son Sky started exploring food with so much passion, devouring his bananas with excitement, I started to dedicate myself to this experiment: banana bread. It turned out so deliciously well, I was amazed. The texture is moist, the sweetness just right. And it fills my kitchen with the alluring aroma of freshly baked goods. My family and friends love it and I hope you do, too.

- 4 large very ripe bananas
- ⅞ cup/200 ml fresh almond milk (page 44)
- 1 cup/120 g buckwheat flour
- 1½ heaped tablespoons organic expeller-pressed coconut oil
- 1 teaspoon ground cinnamon
- ⅛ teaspoon baking soda
- pinch of sea salt (I use Maldon)
- 1 cup/100 g rolled oats (gluten-free if desired)
- 1¼ cups/100 g unsweetened shredded coconut
- 1–2 handfuls raw walnuts

Preheat the oven to 350°F/180°C and line a 9 by 5-inch/23 by 12-cm loaf pan with parchment paper. Combine three bananas, the almond milk, buckwheat flour, coconut oil, cinnamon, baking soda, and sea salt in a high-speed blender and process on high speed until smooth. Add the oats and coconut and pulse a few times until blended. Stir in the walnuts and pour the batter into the pan. Slice the remaining banana lengthwise and place the halves on the batter.

Bake for about 40 minutes. (Check after 30 minutes; a toothpick inserted in the center of the loaf should come out with moist crumbs clinging to it.) Let it cool a bit at room temperature before slicing. I know it's very tempting but it's important to wait!

Note: You can store the banana bread in an airtight container or kitchen towel in the fridge up to three days. I like to toast it and spread any nut butter onto it (page 106). So delicious!

LAZY SUNDAY
OVENBAKED PANCAKE

SIMPLE AND GOOD

───────────────

This recipe was created by accident. We were expecting guests on supershort notice on a superlazy Sunday afternoon. Being me, I always need to offer something deliciously homemade with love and cannot simply buy something not knowing what's inside. I made this within minutes out of whatever I could find in my pantry. It turned out really well…simple and satisfying, and you could just taste that it was made with love.

• 3 tablespoons organic expeller-pressed coconut oil, plus more for greasing the pan
• 5 tablespoons chia seeds
• ⅞ cup/200 ml filtered water
• 1¼ cups/300 ml fresh almond milk (page 44)
• 1¼ cups/150 g buckwheat flour
• ⅞ cup/80 g rolled oats (gluten-free if desired)
• 3–4 tablespoons pure maple syrup or raw coconut nectar, plus more for serving
• 1 teaspoon ground cinnamon
• ½ teaspoon ground vanilla bean powder
• pinch of sea salt (I use Maldon)
• 1¼ cups/180 g blueberries or any berries of your choice

Preheat the oven to 350°F/180°C. Grease a 9-inch/23-cm pie plate with coconut oil. Mix the chia seeds with 1¼ cups/200 ml water in a bowl and set aside for about 15 minutes until they form a thick gel. Combine the almond milk, buckwheat flour, oats, maple syrup, cinnamon, vanilla powder, sea salt, and coconut oil in a high-speed blender and blend on high speed until smooth. Add the chia gel and blend again until thick and creamy. Transfer the batter into the pie plate and swirl in the blueberries. Bake for 40 to 45 minutes or until a toothpick inserted in the center comes out clean. Serve with maple syrup.

Note: You can also serve the pancake with any nut or seed butter (page 106) or Macadamia Vanilla Ricotta (page 100).

PISTACHIO-COCONUT COOKIES

SO EASY AND QUICK TO MAKE

These cookies are quite popular with the kids who come to our house. I always see them leave with a smile and I am one happy chef/mom knowing that they had a healthy, sweet treat.

- ½ cup/90 g pistachio nuts
- 2 ripe bananas
- 1⅞ cups/150 g unsweetened shredded coconut
- 1 tablespoon organic expeller-pressed coconut oil
- pinch of ground vanilla bean powder
- pinch of sea salt (I use Maldon)

Preheat the oven to 350°F/180°C and line a baking sheet with parchment paper. Toast the pistachios until fragrant, let cool, and chop coarsely. Set aside one-third.

Combine the bananas, coconut, coconut oil, vanilla powder, and sea salt in a high-speed blender and blend on high speed until creamy. Use the tamper to push the ingredients into the blades. Transfer the mixture to a bowl and stir in two-thirds of the pistachios.

Form 10 even balls with your hands and roll them in the remaining one-third of the pistachios. Place the balls on the baking sheet and gently press them down with a spatula until you have even disks. Bake for 10 to 15 minutes until the cookies are slightly brown on the outside and soft on the inside. Let cool.

RED VELVET BROWNIES

THE BEAUTY OF BEETS: COLOR, TASTE, AND VERSATILITY!

I love using beets in many savory recipes. Adding beets to baked goods is just a fantastic way to use them as well: they add natural sweetness, density, and body.

- 3 tablespoons organic expeller-pressed coconut oil, plus more for greasing the pan and drizzling the beets
- 1 large beet (9 oz/250 g), peeled and cut into chunks
- 1 cup/250 ml fresh almond milk (page 44)
- 12 large, juicy Medjool dates, pitted
- ⅞ cup/100 g buckwheat flour
- 10 tablespoons/100 g teff flour
- ½ teaspoons baking powder (see note below)
- 1 teaspoon ground vanilla bean powder
- pinch of ground cinnamon
- pinch of sea salt (I use Maldon)

Preheat the oven to 350°F/180°C. Grease a 9-inch/23-cm square baking pan with coconut oil. Spread the beet chunks out on a baking sheet, drizzle with coconut oil, and bake until soft, 15 to 20 minutes. Let cool.

Combine the almond milk, dates, and coconut oil in a high-speed blender and process on high speed until smooth. Add the beet chunks and blend again until combined and creamy. Combine the buckwheat flour, teff flour, baking powder, vanilla powder, cinnamon, and sea salt in a bowl. Add the flour mixture to the blender and blend everything until smooth. Pour the batter into the baking pan and bake for about 25 minutes, making sure not to overbake them. A toothpick inserted in the center should come out with moist crumbs clinging to it. You want your red velvet brownies to be moist and sticky inside.

Notes: When purchasing baking powder, look for an aluminum-free, non-GMO product for the healthiest option possible. (If you are following a gluten-free diet, check the labels to make sure it is gluten-free as well.) I recommend making your own baking powder to make sure you know what's inside. ¼ teaspoon baking soda + ½ teaspoon cream of tartar = 1 teaspoon baking powder

I like to serve Red Velvet Brownies with Macadamia Vanilla Ricotta (page 100). You can also enjoy them with your favorite plant-based ice cream or even with Cashew Sour Cream (page 138).

BLINIS

A TRIP DOWN MEMORY LANE

These delicious blinis—we used to call them oladushki—make me indulge in reminiscences of my childhood and of my beloved Babuschka, who raised me with warmth and unconditional love.I remember those special sleepovers at her home when I woke up in the morning, the kitchen was already filled with the sweet scent of baked oladushki. We snuggled up in our pj's, she told me fairy tales (she was the best at it!), and I slowly enjoyed these sweet mini pancakes. I changed the original recipe, which was based on a lot of things I wouldn't want to eat today, and made my own, way healthier, version. The scent and taste are very much the same, though. Today I am enjoying them with my son Sky, snuggled up in our pj's.

- ⅞ cup/200 ml fresh almond milk (page 44)
- 2 large ripe bananas
- 1 tablespoon organic expeller-pressed coconut oil, plus more for greasing the pan
- 1 teaspoon ground cinnamon
- ½ teaspoon ground vanilla bean powder
- ⅞ cup/100 g buckwheat flour
- ⅓ cup/30 g rolled oats (gluten-free if desired)
- 2 tablespoons/10 g unsweetened shredded coconut
- pinch of sea salt (I use Maldon)

Combine the almond milk, bananas, coconut oil, cinnamon, and vanilla powder in a high-speed blender and process on high speed until smooth. Add the buckwheat flour, oats, coconut, and sea salt. Blend again until thick and creamy.

Grease a frying pan with coconut oil and heat well over medium heat. Use a tablespoon to portion the batter onto the pan (I normally fit four blinis in my pan). Cook the blinis until golden brown on each side and serve.

Note: There are many wonderful toppings you can enjoy with those blinis:
Strawberry Rose Jam (page 94), any Basic Nut + Seed Butter (page 106), Heavenly Chocolate Butter (page 104), Macadamia Vanilla Ricotta (page 100), or simply some pure maple syrup or raw honey.

IT'S ABOUT
ABUNDANCE,
THE JOY
OF EATING
AND THE
CELEBRATION
OF THE
WONDERFUL
PRODUCE
NATURE HAS
TO OFFER.

INDEX

THE TEAM

MIRJAM KNICKRIEM - PHOTOGRAPHY
WWW.MIRJAMKNICKRIEM.DE

STEPHEN PARIS - DESIGN
WWW.STEPHEN-PARIS.COM

Mirjam Knickriem is a photographer based in Berlin. After earning a master's degree in architecture she decided to follow her passion and pursue a career in photography. She moved to New York, where she worked as an assistant to the acclaimed photographer Michael Thompson.

Mirjam's approach to the craft is a combination of storytelling in pictures that capture authenticity and liveliness and working with the colors, light, and scenery that inspire her most. She is always interested to look behind the surface, working closely with people or objects, and always intent to show their inner beauty and realness. She has been capturing colorful and sensual images of Liora Bels for the past 10 years. Mirjam Knickriem is the author and photographer of *Mein Mali*—which showcases the beauty and dignity of the Malian people, and the proceeds of which help to build schools in Mali. She has photographed three other illustrated books.

Berlin native, designer, art director, and brand consultant Stephen Paris has had the pleasure of working with clients from the music and fashion industry as well as from the fields of sports, yoga, and lifestyle, among others. He not only provides design and creative direction but also specializes in branding and marketing.

Stephen pursues his work with passion, and his sense for aesthetics and design brings projects visually to life. It's the fusion between his expertise and the creative desires and authenticity of his clients that he enjoys the most; it's the process of development and growth that inspires him. Working together closely with Liora Bels opened doors to the beauty and bounty of nature and food, which Stephen has vibrantly reflected in his aesthetic design for *The Mix*.

ABOUT THE AUTHOR

Liora Bels is a health food chef, certified nutrition expert, and a food & style consultant. Liora's philosophy is rooted in a holistic approach and she strongly believes that a conscious lifestyle and a healthy cuisine have a great, positive impact on our overall well-being and can ensure a better future.

During her time living abroad for many years and her travels around the world, she gained valuable insights and cultivated her long-sowed fascination with nutrition and healthy food. In her recipes, she embraces the different aromas, food traditions, and aesthetic presentations of the cuisines she encountered. Her love for natural food and cooking combined with her deep interest in its beneficial effects and healing aspects, as well as her hunger for knowledge, led her to devote herself to this career path. *The Mix* is her first book.

Find out more about Liora at:
www.liorabels.com

GRATITUDE

The art of eating well and living a conscious lifestyle has always been dear to my heart. After years of travel, living abroad, and cultural as well as aesthetic and culinary inspiration, I nourished my fascination for nutrition. I chose to deepen my dedication by broadening my knowledge. It is truly a blessing to be able to say that I found my calling, and I have never been happier or more fulfilled in my life and in my work.
I have come a long way in getting to know and nurture myself, in finding the courage to make and accept changes and surrender to the unknown. I embrace the process and enjoy the beauty of becoming. By living a mindful life, making conscious choices, and being thoughtful about what I eat, I honor these blessings through the celebration of healthful daily rituals.

I am beyond grateful for all the inspiration, love, and guidance I have received along the way and my vision is to inspire and move others. To be part of something that makes a difference in their lives.

Writing this cookbook was only possible with the endless support and help of my family, my dearest friends, and my talented team. I express my deepest gratitude for your love, warmth, positivity, generosity of time, and for always believing in me.

To my beloved Babuschka, Hanna Blume, thank you from the depth of my heart and soul for your unconditional love and for teaching me everything about values and being a mensch and for reminding me how much goodness there is in this world.

To my wonderful children, Sky and my baby boy who is growing inside of me, thank you for giving my heart a home. I feel blessed and honored to be your mommy. It is beyond precious. Thank you for your love and patience and for inspiring me to be a better person. Thank you for joining me on this incredible food journey. I am the happiest, luckiest woman on earth.

Thank you dearly, my love Alexis, for your endless support and love and for encouraging me in following this path and profession in the first place. Your compassionate heart, your gentleness and innate humbleness ground me. Thank you for always reminding me of who I am and helping me believe what I am capable of. You are my home.

To my beloved sister Benjamina, you are a witness to my life and I am beyond grateful. Thank you for your belief in me, for your loving support, and for encouraging me to never give up. I love you from the depth of my heart.

A deep thanks to my wonderful family members Ruven, Philip, Eden, and Henry.

I'd like to express my deepest gratitude to my wonderful friends Anne, Andrea, Tiala, Yeliz, Anna, Leontien, and Olivera. You are a very important part of my life. Thank you for filling my journey with your love, smiles, and warmth, your beautiful souls, your wittiness and intelligence, and for encouraging me to live my dreams. I am truly wealthy and blessed having you by my side and in my life. I love you all dearly—words cannot express.

Thank you, Gisela Lüdemann for your warmhearted guidance throughout all these years. I am beyond grateful.

Thank you Karina and Fruit Shop Berlin for your expertise and support.

To my amazing team:
I am so lucky to have very talented and creative experts by my side who have helped me realize my vision and have made this cookbook come to life.

To my wonderful photographer and friend, Mirjam Knickriem, thank you for capturing colorful and sensual images of me throughout special moments of my life for the past ten years. Priceless. Your keen sense of my style and authenticity helped me express my passion for food. Your images are truly beautiful and captivating.

Thank you, Stephen Paris, for your artistic vision, for sharing the same sense of aesthetics as my own, and for translating my vision and passion into a beautiful visual language.

Thank you, dear Nicola Steinigeweg, for being a wonderful assistant and for bringing so much joy and warmth to the project.

Thanks to the teNeues Team Regina Denk and Nadine Weinhold, for your trust and for making this book come to life.

TO MY CHILDREN
— THE NOW, THE FUTURE.
TO LIFE.

IMPRINT

© 2016 teNeues Media GmbH & Co. KG, Kempen

Texts by Liora Bels

Photos by © 2016 Mirjam Knickriem. All rights reserved

Design & layout by Stephen Paris
Copy editing by Cheryl Redmond
Editorial management by Nadine Weinhold
Production by Dieter Haberzettl
Proofing by Jens Grundei & Robert Kuhlendahl

Published by teNeues Publishing Group

teNeues Media GmbH + Co. KG
Am Selder 37, 47906 Kempen, Germany
Phone: +49 (0)2152 916 0
Fax: +49 (0)2152 916 111
e-mail: books@teneues.com

Press department: Andrea Rehn
Phone: +49 (0)2152 916 202
e-mail: arehn@teneues.com

teNeues Publishing Company
7 West 18th Street, New York, NY 10011, USA
Phone: +1 212 627 9090
Fax: +1 212 627 9511

teNeues Publishing UK Ltd.
12 Ferndene Road, London SE24 0AQ, UK
Phone: +44 (0)20 3542 8997

teNeues France S.A.R.L.
39, rue des Billets, 18250 Henrichemont, France
Phone: +33 (0)2 48 26 93 48
Fax: +33 (0)1 70 72 34 82

www.teneues.com

ISBN: 978-3-8327-3381-0
Library of Congress Control Number: 2016942250
Printed in Spain by Estellaprint

Bibliographic information published by
the Deutsche Nationalbibliothek.
The Deutsche Nationalbibliothek lists this
publication in the Deutsche Nationalbibliografie;
detailed bibliographic data are available on
the Internet at http://dnb.dnb.de.

The health advice presented in this book is intended
only as an informative resource guide to help you
make informed decisions; it is not meant to replace
the advice of a physician or to serve as a guide to
self-treatment. Always seek competent medical
help for any health condition.